OPENING A WINDOW
TO THE SOUL

✧

Vern & Carolyn!
Many blessings
on your soul journeys!.
Daryl

OPENING A WINDOW TO THE SOUL

A Guide to Living
Beyond the Human Drama

DAERYL HOLZER

A SOULSHIFT
PUBLICATION

FIRST EDITION
First Printing, 2008

Cover design and artwork by Daeryl Holzer

Library of Congress Control Number: 2008900373
Holzer, Daeryl L., 1958—
Opening a window to the soul: a guide to living beyond the
 human drama / Daeryl Holzer.
p.   cm.
ISBN: 1-4196-8840-5
ISBN-13: 97-81419688409

Printed in the United States

A SoulShift Publication

If you wish to contact the author or order books, please write to
Daeryl Holzer, P.O. Box 1496, Marfa, TX 79843
Visit the author online at www.soulshift.com

This book is dedicated to those
who have sought my guidance.

"The insights that I received from Daeryl's teachings about the soul journey were instrumental in my finally being able to forgive those who had hurt me in this lifetime."

– K.G., Arizona

"This information is distilled and easy to understand. You've given us years of metaphysical research on a platter!"

– J.C., New Mexico

"I treasure your messages. Your insights inspire and guide me... helping me to turn down the editor in my head and amplify my heart and soul voice."

– R.D., Tokyo, Japan

"I am so much more at peace and much less attached to some of the things that were driving me to excess action, worry, and frustration!"

– S.M., California

CONTENTS

OPENING A WINDOW
TO THE SOUL

BEGINNING

My soul journey in this lifetime began in a family that did not believe in God. This was perfectly acceptable to me. I was loved and supported as I learned the practical aspects of living, the value of questioning ideas and reliance on my own merits. The atheist perspective brought a healthy suspicion of organized religion but did nothing to help me understand my inner sense of "something" beyond what I could see or feel or describe, nor my unconscious longing to connect with it.

From an early age I had a sensitivity, a subtle knowing, which often did not fit my conscious understanding or the experiences of others in my world. My perceptions confused me. Thinking people were speaking cruel words out loud, I realized later that I was just "hearing" their intense, emotional thoughts. Because I "knew" something from a conversation I had not participated in, people tended to be annoyed or distrustful toward me. I sensed my playmates' pain or sadness as if it were my own and believed that I was responsible. It was unclear why or how, but I knew I was different.

I also had a vague awareness of something vast and profound, which I could not express, an elusive presence just beyond my reach. I touched upon the mystery in certain moments when I painted or worked with my hands creatively, or when running or dancing to the point where a surge of extra vibrancy flowed through me. Once, immersed in my existence as "someone somewhere else," I pretended to be an Indian and built a domed shelter with ivy strands woven through the long clippings from a plum tree. I stripped naked to better decorate my skin with the staining colors of grass, Pyracantha berries, and yarrow. Upon discovery, I was shocked back into my seven-year-old self, unaware of how I "knew" how to do these things.

I had a longing to understand life beyond the rational, physical world and to become connected with the mystery, whatever it was. So as a young adult, I began to explore esoteric belief systems and alternate realities. The psychedelic culture of the 70's introduced me to "the unspoken thing," to connections and perceptions that happened in a fluid way, beyond the intellectual mind. I studied ancient metaphysical societies, native religions and rituals, and eastern philosophies.

I had personal experiences with inexplicable phenomenon: ghosts, power spots, prophetic dreams, and magical occurrences. Learning astrology and tarot systems gave me a new way of delving into the patterns behind human behavior. I met others who were more like me and learned skills to work with what I finally understood to be my clairvoyant gifts.

All of this was fascinating and enriching and opened my eyes to the limitless variety of human lifestyles and beliefs. But I was still frustrated, as if I were trying to put together a jigsaw puzzle with many of the pieces missing. There had to be something more. I could sense it, but it was apparently beyond my grasp.

I turned to a more traditional path by moving my freelance graphic design career into a corporate job. I tried to pretend that having a house and husband would make me feel whole. Instead, I became increasingly dissatisfied as I realized that my days were filled with superficial appearances and power struggles. Not only was it not enough, but maintaining the illusion of a fine normal life left me exhausted. I felt like I was trapped in a box while everything of true value was outside of that box.

My soul screamed for a change, but I was too afraid to shift out of the comfort zone of doing what I was "supposed" to do. I was paralyzed as a deer in headlights, knowing that to stay still would be to die yet unable to move, even as I watched danger approaching.

Clinging to the belief that if only I tried a little harder my life would improve, I pushed myself until my physical and emotional stamina snapped. Injuring my back at work set in motion a domino sequence of events. With a mixture of denial and resistance, plus the determination to hang on, I tried to deal with the loss of my health, my job, and the sense of identity I held through my career. Lying on my back in pain, and without the distraction of work, I woke up to how emotionally hollow and abusive my marriage had become. I also began to notice that there was something terribly wrong when my young daughter was left alone with her father. Breaking free of the control and manipulation that had grown unchecked in our home was traumatic and depleting, but my bubble of denial was finally burst. As the divorce was finalized, I felt released from years of unhealthy enmeshment, but I also no longer had a home, a career, security, or any money.

Stripped down to the bare bones of my soul, I was forced to question who I was beyond the trappings of my human condition. The question "What am I here for?" became my focus. Convincing myself that my losses were an opportunity to start fresh, I embraced my new life with an attitude of liberation and excitement. But I was terrified. Could I really step out of that box? Was something terrible going to happen if I dared to become more?

As part of the process of coping with a major life transition, I began to work with a therapist who used traditional concepts as well as alternative approaches. Initially addressing the issue of divorce, we shifted to exploration of my back injury (as it had been the catalyst for all the rest).

I had no idea of the phenomenal shift that was about to take place.

I was guided on a journey during a hypnotherapy regression, where I found myself experiencing life in the body of an old man. My room of stone was ringed with shelves holding herbs in glass jars. A long table was crowded with large leather-bound books, pages filled with handwritten symbols and notations describing my herbal healing and astrology research. The scene shifted to me being dragged into the dusty street by an angry mob, sent by the church, in opposition to my spiritual beliefs and practices. When a wooden staff came down on my lower back, I felt a "crack!" at the spot of my current injury, like a button being pressed and sending sympathetic resonance down my legs. I realized in that moment that my back pain was sourced in more than just my current life.

I witnessed my soul leaving that body as a result of paralyzing injuries. I anguished at the loss of life and unjust persecution, but the greatest despair was for the loss of such a huge body of knowledge that had been accumulated during a long and studious life devoted to the healing arts. From the altered perspective of hypnotherapy, I was able to clearly evaluate and process past life events that were still affecting me. It was like film from two movies playing at the same time, with similar sequences of events overlapping and blending. With guidance from the therapist, I was able to understand how my unpopular esoteric beliefs (as the old man) had led to death in that time, and had seeded my current *fear* that it could happen again. I had been avoiding a spiritual path in present time as though that same danger was still real.

As the therapist helped me to let go of these associations, I felt a pulsing aliveness tingling down my legs, as if nerves were being turned back on. Later, when I stood up, I was without pain or limitation of movement. My physical healing had begun.

Toward the end of the session, the therapist asked me to look deeper asking, "Is it really true that all this information is lost?" I flashed back to the moment of my soul leaving the old man's body. A presence appeared, like a little fairy "Tinkerbell," bringing me a gleeful message. "Nothing is lost. We have been holding onto all of your knowledge, just waiting for you to reclaim it!" I didn't understand until later exactly "who" she was or what that meant, but my sense of loss and despair was gone.

Perhaps most importantly, I gained the awareness that I had lived more times than just now, that what I might not remember from other lives *could* affect me in this one, and that I had the power to change my life simply by looking at my existence from the soul perspective.

Since that awakening, I have been more comfortable with being different, with exploring and expressing my unconventional ideas. And, finally, I began using my gifts to help other people by teaching workshops, giving clairvoyant readings and doing past life regressions. I was making the shift from graphic designer to healer with a decent level of success, but without the confidence I needed to do it full time. When I was able to put my self-doubt aside, I trusted what I was "seeing." Clients gave me positive feedback that the information was helpful, but I felt that I was trying to do something really hard, all alone.

I was attracted to spiritual teachers and channelers, in hopes that they could provide answers to my questions and guide me to a deeper awareness of my own intuitive abilities. I had experience with people who had a strong connection to some kind of higher wisdom, but who distorted the information to suit their own purposes. The fallible human personality led many of these "spiritual leaders" to operate with a lack of integrity, hidden agendas, and often, a need to have power over others. The whole idea of finding a teacher became tainted and twisted, and I anguished over my desire to have direct access to Spirit for advice I could trust.

I was also still struggling with the pain of my divorce, wondering how long I would have to endure being so wounded and emotionally needy, when an offer to join my two closest friends in Hawaii came. I jumped at the chance for retreat and was hopeful of renewal.

There, due to an unusual dream, my life took an amazing turn.

In the dream, I heard a phone ringing, and when I answered it, a soft female voice said, "Hello. This is Taliana." She was matter of fact, as though she expected me to recognize her voice. "Do I know you?" I asked. With friendly assurance she explained, "Oh, yes! We have known each other many lifetimes, and I am here to help you do your work."

As she spoke to me in the dream, I became aware of a warmth, as though there was a wave of cleansing energy swirling through my body from head to toe. I was overcome with a profound sense of peace and comfort, like the relief a baby feels at being held by its mother – complete unconditional love. I asked her, "What is this feeling?"

"This is how you are all meant to feel. Anytime you want to connect, just call my name and I will be with you."

I woke up. Eyes wide open in the dark, I mentally reviewed the dream, intent upon remembering every detail. In the morning, my mind bouncing between skepticism and delight, I spoke her name in my head, "Taliana." Like taking a deep breath, the rush of bliss once again filled me, expanding my heart, relaxing every cell in my being.

As I described this dream to my friends, their enthusiasm and trust was so powerful and infectious that it didn't occur to me to say "no" when they encouraged me to call her in. I shut my eyes and spoke her name.

A flood of questions: "Who is Taliana? Why have you come to Daeryl? What's Daeryl's soul purpose? What's *my* soul purpose?"

Explanations flowed, not from my mind, but from a vast source, far away, yet deep within my soul. There was nothing uncomfortable, no fear of giving up control. I had a sense of "I'm not alone doing this," so I kept going. We learned that Taliana was a soul family member who had been with me in another lifetime, a time when we had worked together as healers and teachers. She was to be my direct access to Spirit, to the knowledge in my own soul, and my ultimate source of love and wisdom. For this life, we also have a soul agreement to work together, for her to help me with my soul path of teaching and sharing, but this time I am in the physical and she is not.

I was astonished to be speaking these words and realized that for once my "busy little monkey mind" was totally out of the way!

I cannot explain why, but this turn of events seemed both exceedingly bizarre and perfectly natural. My veil of self-doubt dissolved as I embraced my reunion with something magnificent, something familiar that I had been separated from long ago. As I worked with this new connection to Spirit, for myself, and for others, I came to know, deep in my heart, the wholeness I had been seeking my entire life.

Before Taliana, I had known what it felt like to make a connection with the sacred, to feel the mystery moving within me, and I had learned how to access information with my clairvoyant skills, but I had not experienced *both* simultaneously! By calling in Taliana, no matter *what* she was, I was tapping into the sublime *and* accessing intelligent, conversational explanations. Up until now, I had just been putting my toe in the water; this was a full dive!

I returned to my work with clients filled with confidence and enthusiasm; the energy moving through me coated all my words in a warm loving presence and the delivery of information became more exalted. I had people tell me that they felt the presence of something they did not recognize as me. The challenge for me, still the skeptic, was to accept what was happening. My first inclination was resistance, timidness and not wanting to reveal that I could do this special thing. This creeps in on me still, as I often question what I am doing... until I call her in, and then it feels natural.

Working with this connection to Spirit, I began to get clarity and understanding of my life and others around me from a soul perspective, with compassion and grace. I became less emotionally needy in love relationships, less frantic in fear. Instead of panicking in stressful situations, I was able to stay calm and grounded. I was given guidance that, when followed, led me to amazing transformations within myself as well as in my external circumstances.

Just when I thought life was improving, another series of intense personal challenges arose to test the spiritual wisdom and practical tools I was gathering. For the next six years, I struggled to remain centered, loving, and strong as I faced a mother's worst nightmare – my teenaged daughter was in severe crisis. Before unraveling and healing what was at the core of her overwhelming pain and confusion, she and I both struggled through her suicide attempts, running away, substance abuse, hospitalization, and treatment programs. We endured additional trauma trying to do the right thing in the midst of custody battles, Social Services interventions, and directives from medical professionals.

There were times when I didn't know where she was or what might be happening to her, when my vivid imagination would paint an image of the worst thing possible. There were times when I could not help her because someone else (street kids, social workers, psychiatrists, lawyers, or ex-husband) had more control than I did. Just when I had adjusted to being forced to let go, it would become necessary to step back in and take care of business at a moment's notice. I never knew if she was going to push me away, blame me, or beg for rescue. Powerlessness was in my face, but my love and faith in her was fierce. I never stopped caring and remained devoted to holding the vision that she (and I) would get through this.

We were blessed with tremendous support from family and friends and developed greater understanding and healing through traditional therapies. Even so, without the clarity and peace I received through my connection to Spirit, and the ability to see what was happening from a soul level, I could easily have fallen to pieces, been swallowed in bitterness or despair, or lashed out with vengeful frustration.

Instead, I was able to focus on the soul paths and challenges involved beyond the appearance of human dramas and conflicts. I held unshakable faith that all of the human pain and injustice was exactly what was necessary for our soul journey. I felt so much "back up" of love and acceptance from my guides that I found the strength to love myself in spite of my weaknesses. I had tools to access peace in the midst of chaos, to create miracles in the midst of dire need, and to remain reasonable when everyone around me was acting crazy.

Now I see the blessings that were laid open at every step of the ordeal, on so many levels and for so many people, and especially for my daughter who has achieved an amazing level of empowered wisdom, self-worth and joy.

After this life experience and personal healing, my client work became more effective. I was now equipped with wisdom that could show someone a way to dance through a challenge without feeling like a victim, or hating somebody, or doing "the wrong thing." I could honestly say I knew what they were feeling, and tell them what had worked for me. Because of my own personal growth, I became more confident that my own issues were not getting in the way of what I was "seeing" for someone else, and I lost attachment to whether someone took my advice or not.

Through my own experience with Taliana, and other guides, I learned the value of living not as a separate entity, but as a team with Spirit. From no other source had I been able to access such trustworthy guidance and unconditional support, at any moment, in any situation. Nothing else had enabled me to make such profound shifts in my consciousness, my relationships and my ability to live well.

There were times while writing this book when I would struggle with a way to explain a certain concept. I might be unclear about what was true, or not see a way out of a human struggle. It was inevitable then that a situation or challenge would arise in my own life, or a client would present a dilemma, relating to my uncertainty. In that need, and because I was asking, an outpouring of clarity and solutions would present themselves. No doubt, my guides (or my higher soul) were at work providing a vehicle for me to access the higher wisdom I had locked inside.

Allowing my guides to "play" with me in this game, I've shifted from just gritting my teeth and getting through life, to embracing my soul's journey with confidence and enthusiasm. Now that who I am and what I am doing here is no longer the mystery it once was, my focus turns to joyfully sharing my soul's reclaimed knowledge.

The information in this book is my attempt to encapsulate and explain my understanding of who we are and what we are doing here – and what "here" even is. Utilizing these tools and perspectives has proven to be very effective, for my own healing and development as well as for clients. For over fifteen years, the skeptic in me has been "testing" the validity of these ideas and concepts, and I am constantly amazed and assured as I witness consistent and powerful results. It now seems less important to me whether or not something can be "proven" than whether or not something helps.

The book is set up in a question and answer format to mimic the rhythm of a client session. It is useful to be able to ask, "what about this?" and get an explanation. The questions are a compilation of voices – clients, students, friends, myself – asking for clarity and advice. The answers are a blending of direct responses from my guides with that of my wise woman voice. The knowledge base that comes through is the wisdom that I have accumulated, through clairvoyant spirit knowing, studying and reading, and traveling my own rocky road. The examples used to support explanations are actual client experiences or my own.

There are no answers or directives, only explanations and responses. My intention is to provide information to help people make better choices for themselves through deeper understanding of the soul story behind common situations. There may be several suggestions in any scenario: a way to accept it, a way to be patient with it, a way to move away from it, a way to change it. The choice of "what to do" is always a matter of individual free will.

Throughout the book, I resist using spiritual terms such as God, Heaven, Angels, etc. because they are somewhat limiting and are tied to specific belief systems. I am not interested in challenging a person's religion or viewpoint. I am simply offering a new perspective, an avenue for people to connect to Spirit in a personal, powerful way, beyond what they may be currently aware of, or used to.

The ability to call in Spirit guides, to have a profound connection with Spirit, is not particularly special or unique to me. We are each meant to feel connected and blended, rather than alone, on our Earth journey. It is my hope that the information and scenarios that follow will help you to open the window to your soul and to live beyond your own human drama with clarity and delight.

THE SOUL

You are more than your body, your thoughts, or your feelings.

I sense a presence of something, a life force that I cannot see or touch or explain. I get a glimpse of it sometimes, just beyond my self, and sometimes, I feel it deep within me. What is this other?

You are having awareness of the nature of the Universe, as a vast and never-ending essence of all existence, a pulsing vibration of energy. You are perceiving a quality of your own being which embodies that same Universal nature, the part of you that is more than just the thinking, doing, feeling aspect of your human self. You are recognizing your soul.

What is a soul?

The soul is the consistently unique aspect of a person that lives on beyond the human form. As individual as a fingerprint, it is the part of you that is "alive," as a vital life force, whether you have a body or not.

Souls are as drops of water originating from a universal and vast ocean. Each drop of water, though unique in its own way, has the exact same properties and is made of the same stuff as that ocean. Each drop is an individualized expression of the cumulative mass of drops with the same life-giving nature. There is no difference of quality between the drop of water and the ocean, only a difference in volume.

Just like that drop from the ocean never stops being water, the soul essence exists, whether in human form on Earth or not. Your Soul encompasses the richness of all that you have ever been and the vast potential of all you dare to become.

What does it mean to have a soul?

Soul essence brings an awareness of the mysterious life force energy beyond its own reality. It is the ability to feel and know, "I am not all there is." With the physical reality of Earthly perceptions, there is attention to difference: the self, others like self, and others not like self. The soul returns awareness to "oneness."

Even if you do not have conscious awareness, your soul still operates. It is the part of you that longs for emotional bonds and social relationships – the soul remembers the unlimited blending and connection of the non-physical realm. It is the part that seeks for purpose and meaning to life rather than being satisfied with the mundane task of living – the soul remembers why it has come here. It is the part that assigns human characteristics to the unseen mystery – the soul remembers its "sameness" to *all that is.*

The soul aspect allows a person to grasp that there was something before the current life, and that there will be something afterward. Remembering your place in the big picture moves you from existing as an inconsequential or limited human, to thriving in communion with Universal Soul and Spirit.

What do you mean by Universal Soul and Spirit?

Universal Soul is a term describing the cumulative mass of energies of all souls – the collective soul essence of all human beings in a pure and exalted state. Free from the personality traits or frailties of the human condition, the Universal Soul is capable of unconditional love. Each of us, whether currently in a body or not, is part of the Universal Soul. There is never any separation from it. As that single soul is like a drop of water, the Universal Soul is like the ocean.

Spirit is the infinite magnificence of the Universe, the vibration at the core of all existence. Having no bounds or limits, it is *all* and *nothing* blended in perfect unison and creating a movement of energy everywhere. Existing at the heart of everything, there is nothing out of harmony with it and no separation from it. Though many have tried to define or prove their version, souls have a variety of uniquely individual responses to this vibration and so description will always be a subjective interpretation in accordance with the level of a soul's development and comprehension. There are many names for this "Nameless One" – in this book, Spirit.

Though more intangible in the physical plane, both Universal Soul and Spirit flow readily throughout both the Earth and Spirit realms.

What do you mean by Spirit realm?

Spirit realm describes that which is beyond the physical reality of Earth. Though not really a place in the way that Earth is a place (where the concepts of space and time exist), it can be thought of as the link between all that is in the physical realm and all that is not. The Spirit realm is the "home" for souls who are between human lives. In the Spirit realm, all souls are automatically immersed in the unity of Universal Soul, with direct access to the Infinite, to Spirit.

Why don't souls retain that unity on Earth?

Life on Earth involves having an individualized experience, a "personal" life, rather than one fully blended with Spirit and other souls as it was before birth. The first thing a soul encounters when born into a human body is the nature of physical separation. Immediately, there is a desire for reconnection, a seeking of love and belonging. This shock and anguish over separation is at the heart of all human suffering, but it does not need to be so. Separation is a temporary illusion of the human condition, not a reality of the soul.

It is a matter of remembering that you are part of the Universal Soul instead of experiencing life as being alone.

How does one stay connected to Universal Soul?

Souls begin their sequence of lives with a soul family, a cluster of souls of like frequency who seek to share the Earth experience. Souls maintain a sense of connection and support on a Spiritual level by forming into a soul family, a sub-group of Universal Soul. Some soul family members are in the physical while others are in the Spirit realm. The soul family is the ever-constant link to the unconditional love of Universal Soul, whether a soul is in a body or not.

How does a soul connect to Spirit?

While in the Spirit realm, connection with Spirit is automatic.

As a new baby, a person connects with Spirit by way of the people in their immediate environment. Typically, with parents, the nature of Spirit comes through for that soul as the archetypal energy of Divine Mother and Divine Father, as an expression of the unconditional love and belonging (mother), as well as the safety and abundance (father), that souls experience in their connection to Spirit while in the non-physical. To whatever level the parents are capable of being that and allowing that energy through, a person retains or loses its sense of union with Universal Soul and Spirit.

No matter what the early childhood experience, a person can still access Spirit through Spirit Guides, those members of the soul family who are not presently in human form. As part of the Universal Soul, Spirit Guides provide a direct line to the unlimited love, wisdom and assistance of the cumulative mass of all souls, as well as to Spirit. Spirit Guides are your guides *to* Spirit, as much as they are those in the Spirit realm who "guide" you in life.

Are souls created by Spirit?

Souls are not created so much as they form; like drops of rain before falling to Earth. As microcosmic energies of Spirit, the essence of individualized souls are drawn to each other – like attracts like – and just as raindrops from a cloud do not think, "I want to fall now," they simply do.

Why do souls come to Earth?

I would call it the polarity experiment. Part of the game on Earth is to play with balancing opposites. Day and night, male and female, chaos and order, earth and sky, birth and death, growth and destruction, all give a soul the richness of experience that does not exist in the Spirit realm. In addition to the body type differences of male or female, large or small, healthy or disabled, and the environmental variety of race, language, temperature, and terrain, human souls are able to experiment with how they will live. "What would it be like to be act with aggression versus cooperation? What happens when I am educated and privileged versus poor and oppressed? What is the difference between a life facing hardships and achieving success versus a life of ease and complacency? What is it like to wander about instead of staying in a close community?" Living first one way, and then another, a soul learns through duality. Trying both, comparing and analyzing, in order to achieve balance and understanding.

It is only on the Earth, in a physical form, that a soul can experience "doing" instead of simply "being." Without the body, a soul cannot move, or touch, or express. The body allows a soul to have emotional and tactile sensations, and to immerse itself in the actions and reactions that manifest. Only while in a body can a soul learn the intricacies of cause and effect, influencing changes and improvements, and creating something that was not there before. It is the difference between watching a game and being a player.

The Earth environment also provides the challenge of maintaining a sense of spiritual essence while in a physical plane reality. In comparison to the boundless and fluid energy of the Spirit realm, a soul must come to terms with existing in a limited manner. The adjustment to this new reality is much like a person accustomed to being chauffeured in luxury suddenly stranded alone on a remote road attempting to restart a broken-down jalopy with no tools or knowledge of automobile mechanics.

The soul is now trapped inside a mass of flesh and bone requiring food, water, shelter, and warmth, while being vulnerable to pain, injury, and illness. There is a limitation of consciousness and mental functioning – a human brain and human confusion – rather than the infinite wisdom of the Universal Soul. There is also the frustration of not being able to blend at will with others for comfort and belonging. The challenge is to be able to once again feel the ecstatic freedom of your existence flowing beyond your physical form.

Simultaneously, there can be awareness of oneself as a unique individual, and awareness of unity with Spirit, Universal Soul, and each other. On a pure energy level, we are all one. Our sense of separation is only an illusion of the physical. We can make a choice to have an Earth experience where we feel very alone and shut off, with lots of barriers to being connected. Or we can choose to be open and share the richness of relationships.

All humans are working out the bugs of existence: how

to be in a physical body, how to survive, how to interact with each other, and how to find comfort. We are here to embrace the limitations of the physical plane, to change, grow and adapt.

How do the limitations of time and space influence us?

Time and space only exist within the physical plane and in the context of human existence. These confines are not relevant outside of human perception. They help define the parameters of the earth and the physical reality that makes the human experience different than the Spirit realm. The concept of space and dimension allows you to identify and converse about what is being experienced and what enhances your ability to function logistically.

Time is a human concept. Time does not matter to a mouse, a rock or water. Time is something that is part of the human consciousness, an awareness of which enables a person to measure causes and effects while in the physical.

One of the qualities that set humans apart from other creatures is the ability to improve one's situation. In order to do that, a person needs to be able to analyze what they see and then imagine how it could be some other way. To understand how things change, people need a concept of sequence. "This is how it was *before*, and this is how it is *after*."

Time affects a rock as it is eroded by water or wind, but time only *matters* to humans who need to be able to discern causes and effects in order to evolve. If such conscious development and change were not the nature of humans, you would not pay attention to time.

Do souls come to Earth for just one life?

It is for not just one life, but a series of lifetimes, the number of which varies for each soul. The richness of possibilities to be explored and the diversity of scenarios to balance cannot be achieved within the brief span of a single human life. Only through living one life in extreme of poverty and then another in opulent wealth does a soul balance the challenges of financial abundance. Only through the experience of being victimized does a soul gain compassion and learn not to inflict harm. Much like a human child, it is only through stages of development that a soul can evolve to its highest potential.

What are the stages of development in a soul's evolution?

The evolution of a soul through its many lives is like the image of a tornado, tiny at the base and gradually increasing in volume. It is ever expanding, brighter at the top, in constant motion, with an upward spiraling progression. Symbolically, there are two tones, dark and light, fear and love, confusion and awareness. There is no right or wrong place to be along the spiral. The appearance of dark or light is merely an indication of the stage of progress.

Souls in their earliest human bodies are fairly clueless about life in the material world, especially in regard to getting needs met and relating to one another. The focus is on survival. Driven by self-centered motivations, with little consideration for others or the long-term effects of their actions, they are capable of what our later awareness considers to be incomprehensible and unacceptable behavior.

As a soul evolves, there is less confusion and less repetition of earlier human frailties. A shifting out of primal responses begins, eliminating the choices that don't work.

Following the spiral progression upward through the cycle of lives, there are flashes of light representing more conscious behaviors, moments of insight and spiritual compassion. As a soul learns to balance physical needs with the awareness of others, the overall tone becomes brighter. In the middle, the spiral is an equal blend of dark and light representing a balance of primal and enlightened behavior.

A soul's focus evolves from creating conflicts and challenges to embracing the causes and effects of past experiences, some of which have hurt others, and some of which have only been traumatic to the self. The spiral's brightness increases as a soul shifts towards righting previous mistakes and seeking connection and cooperation.

Eventually, there is more light than dark, more ability to act with compassion and healing than to react from emotions that hurt. Eventually, there is more joy and love than fear and loneliness. Finally, the spiral tornado image is almost pure light with only a few specks of dark from time to time. At this level, a soul will have transcended all restriction and lack and gained a functioning awareness of its Spirit nature and oneness with all. Ultimately, a soul will exist as a limitless being while in the physical.

Are there specific tasks for a particular soul as it goes through its evolution?

For each soul, in any given life, there are two main goals to accomplish. The first we will call personal soul balancing, and the second we will call life purpose. The beginning part of one's life is usually taken up addressing those issues and environmental traumas that occurred in previous lives or childhood, a bit like taking care of unfinished business before you can move on to the greater task of who you have come here to be.

As we have mentioned, the subconscious stores up memories from the past until a person is at a level where they can assimilate what happened. In that regard, the personal soul balancing involves looking back into what has been experienced and sorting it out with others. The soul has the opportunity to make up for short-comings, learn from mistakes by doing things differently, and overcome old fears and emotional patterns. Awareness of what is happening on the soul level brings understanding of the personal lessons involved so that they can be resolved rather than remaining trapped in a belief of karmic penance or suffering ongoing frustration.

Once a soul has accomplished most of its personal balancing, there is a shift towards fulfilling some sort of higher purpose in order to bring greater meaning to life. There is usually a common thread that runs through all lives regarding a given soul's life purpose. It could be a "mission" of healing, leading, bringing wisdom, or creating innovations to advance society. Some souls have an ongoing task of being adversarial – pushing others into growth.

For souls at the beginning of their series of lives, the focus is more on personal growth as there is much to be undone from the "mistakes" that have been made. As they learn more about how to be here in this physical world, fewer interactions cause imbalances, and it becomes easier to resolve previous challenges. Souls then become more driven to find out who they really are and what they are doing here – they become more interested in being of service to others and having some sort of impact here that will bring meaning and purpose to their existence. This is because they are remembering their soul essence, whether they know it or not!

Even with recognition that there is a greater path than mere survival, a person trying to follow their soul's calling may be thwarted until they have addressed the required personal balancing. The burden of carrying too much baggage from the past gets in the way. It is a two-stage process – releasing the old and serving the purpose – certainly with some overlap and the two are related. Much of what is endured in the early mistakes, conflicts and struggles, teaches the compassion, strengths and talents that are needed to accomplish one's purpose. As a soul moves through its cycle of lives and evolves through soul ages of development, there are different proportions of the two tasks. For the youngest of souls, there is a taste of the soul purpose, and even for the oldest of souls, there is a little balancing to do.

Young souls. Old souls. What does that mean?

Some people are the embodiment of souls who have been here many times before, who have experimented with many different ways of being, and who are in more advanced stages of learning and human behavior. Other people are just beginning their cycle of lives here, in the earliest stages of soul development, experimenting with the rawest of human emotions and behavior. Just as a baby – inexperienced and vulnerable – is no less valuable or important than a mature adult, there is no better or worse place for a person to be in their soul age.

The perspective of understanding people – their choices and capabilities – according to their soul age helps you to be less judgmental and less disappointed in others when they do not act the way you would like them to. It is assumed that a baby will be dependent and emotionally impulsive. It is natural for a toddler to not share its toys. It is an appropriate stage of development for a teenager to be self-absorbed and competitive. Just as we cannot expect a child to have the capacity to learn or behave as an adult, we cannot demand that baby and young souls will operate as older souls. Chances are that you will not get your emotional needs met from a baby soul parent. It is equally unlikely to get a young soul, whose focus is competition and winning, to acquiesce in negotiation for the sake of harmony.

Each soul age has certain characteristics, motivations, and challenges. Learning to discern the level of development that a person, or even a culture, is operating from brings insight and a greater ability to resolve differences. This does not mean that you must allow harmful behaviors, but it is important to know whom you are dealing with. Every person is only capable of being what they are at the soul stage of development they are addressing. Understanding what someone else may be striving to accomplish – the individual needs and lessons of their soul – keeps us from getting stuck in a right versus wrong mindset.

Can you give us more information about the soul ages? How are they different?

The growth of a soul through the various stages of development is best described through the analogy of the way a person ages in their human life. Just as a child learns a little more each year, a soul develops gradually through its various lives. The feelings and behaviors, the attitudes and interactions, will be comparable to those of a child growing up into adulthood and old age. Their frame of reference and what motivates a person can be understood by relating to the stage of soul growth they are in. For example, even though a person may be 50 years old, if they are a very young soul, they may express themselves with the emotional demands of a ten-year-old. Likewise, a four-year-old child may deliver astoundingly wise and compassionate advice to her parents, exhibiting the likeliness of being an older soul. Understanding the soul age gives us the ability to anticipate the feelings and motivations of another. No matter how old the human body is, a baby soul is not capable of acting like an old soul, and a mature soul does not think the same way a young one does. Differentiating the various stages of growth is not meant as a tool to judge one as better than the other, but to have greater understanding and reasonable expectations of oneself and others.

The four groups of soul age described below are meant as general categories of a gradual progression, not as hard-lined division or caste ranking. As a soul advances, there are overlaps in the developing traits. Also, there can be leaps of growth as well as relapses. There could be a life where a soul is in the later phases of the young soul development, but then he experiences a lifetime of overwhelming trauma or grave mistakes, requiring him to regress and relearn the lessons involved. Or, a soul could be in the early mature stage and have a huge leap of growth during a single lifetime as a result of mastering a sequence of emotional challenges which launch him directly into the late mature or early old soul stage. The number of lives that it takes to evolve through the soul age stages is individual and ultimately flexible.

Baby souls: In the earliest of lives, souls are just beginning to adapt to life in the physical and have many of the same characteristics as young infants. Baby souls are at the beginning stages of self-awareness and understanding, with a focus on the needs and sensations of the physical body and a limited frame of reference due to lack of experience. Baby souls are just learning what they require for survival, and so are less inclined to think of the good of the group, which may seem self-centered. Like small toddlers, they are not yet able to regulate their emotions, which are felt intensely and shift quickly. They are most comfortable in relationships and environments where the roles and rules are simple, where others are just like them and there are few variations. For the safety of what is familiar, baby souls often incarnate

---

together in clans and small communities with clearly defined and enforced rules for social behavior. Conformity versus diversity brings them security and comfort. Spiritually, there can be a tendency towards primitive beliefs and superstitions. Just like infants, they can be delightfully spontaneous, joyful, and an expression of divine love when they are feeling safe, or screaming out in fear when they are not. The challenge of the baby soul stage is to accumulate experiences in order to learn how things work here, emotionally and physically. The goal is to develop the confidence in oneself which is prerequisite to trying new situations in the future.

Young souls: As souls gain awareness of themselves as separate individuals, they begin to take on the challenges of comparing themselves to others. In contrast to the dependency of the previous stage, the young soul stage focuses on acquiring new skills and knowledge, as well as material possessions for security. Through competition, there is constant evaluation of who is better, who has more, etc. With the somewhat cocky nature of teenagers, souls at this age engage in conflict, overachieving, and intolerance. These are the warriors, the corporate climbers, the wealthy merchants, the politicians and star athletes who need to win at all costs. Spiritually, young souls tend towards organized religion with a missionary or evangelical bent. Sometimes irrational and sometimes calculated, young souls do not yet have the emotional maturity to control impulses or put one's own needs aside for another. But as they experiment with imposing their will on others, they learn that what they do to others will have some effect on them. Though they can be rebellious or overbearing, these are the souls who will take risks and get things done.

Mature souls: As souls move past the challenge of acquiring material possessions and claiming their own self worth in the world, they are able to address emotional factors and broader social concerns. The goal of this stage is to achieve harmonious relationships, which is deemed much more important than competing for status, power, or wealth. A soul develops the ability to feel what another person feels, so that only through mutually positive outcomes is there a sense of success. In order to gain an understanding of self and others, mature souls are drawn to highly charged inter-actions which are often soul agreements for balancing. These are the people that have one tumultuous relationship after another, who are enmeshed with their partners or children, or who get involved in interpersonal dramas that others would avoid. Spiritually, mature souls are attracted to information and groups which help them to understand their interconnectedness – not so much joining as seeking. The lessons of this stage are mastered when a soul learns how to connect deeply without becoming responsible for another's pain or compromising the integrity of either soul. Mature souls have an impact on the world through social and humanitarian concerns in their service to those less fortunate or empowered. Much like the role of parents, mature souls are inclined to take care of people as teacher, social worker, nurse, or emergency service worker. While struggling with their own emotional pain and turmoil, these souls are not afraid to get involved and can bring about much social reform and assistance to others.

Old souls: For the older souls, life here is not so much about interactions or experiences so much as evaluation and introspection. Throughout their many and varied lifetimes, they have gathered the wisdom of experience and have a multifaceted perspective. Since they have most likely "been there, done that" with most situations, they are less judgmental or frustrated by the seemingly intolerable behavior of others. They accept that the world is filled with a wide variety of people and dramas, and seek to rest and review. Like an elder sitting and observing the young children playing, they are amused but not riled. In fact, these are the ones who are often misjudged as lazy or inattentive, simply because they will not get charged up about a situation that a younger soul might deem critical. Rather than take action, they may give sage and compassionate advice. Old souls are most attuned spiritually to individual practices that lead to contemplation and inner peace. The old soul stage is not a time to start new things or entertain conflict, but to resolve unfinished business and make things balanced on a soul level. It is also a time to enjoy harmonious relationships and simply relish the pleasures that can be had here on Earth.

What are some of the goals a soul might be trying to accomplish in any given life?

Though a soul will sometimes choose a particular set up for an entirely new and unfamiliar experience, often the choice is a direct response to the immediately preceding life. Perhaps they need to experience the opposite, for perspective and balance. Or they may repeat a similar setup in order to have a second chance to learn from previous mistakes and do things differently. Sometimes a soul opts for an alternative circumstance but the same challenge to test and reinforce one's recent growth within a new context.

An example of balancing by living in two opposite scenarios is a man who has spent a life focusing on acquiring wealth and power. Though mastering a secure way of being, the cost is that he has missed out on love and intimacy. His next lifetime, he may choose a setting in a very poor family which, though lacking in means, holds great value in caring for each other and being emotionally close. Assimilating the two experiences, this soul learns what has true value in life and can work on integrating prosperity and relationships in the future.

Some goals require a relationship with a particular

person, perhaps the same soul from another life in order to right a wrong that had been done. Other life choices are more about acquiring a particular strength or quality; the environment becomes more important than the individuals who interact in the experience. It doesn't matter who teaches you, just that someone does.

So vast is the diversity of the human population – different physical bodies, personalities, beliefs, social status, and community structures – that the opportunity to take on any given challenge is always readily available.

A soul can experience everything from being a wealthy tribal elder in a remote mountain settlement, to a poor disabled orphan in a crowded metropolis. They can experiment with mastering an infinite number of human talents; from gaining the skills and knowledge required to subsist on semiarid farmland to discovering new and profound scientific advancements in a sophisticated research laboratory.

Who decides what lessons are needed or where a soul is to go? Who picks the setting, body, family, etc.?

There is not some other being choosing for a soul, but rather, they are guided through a process of evaluation and selection. Before birth in the physical, a soul is merged with those in its soul family who give support, and it is from this cumulative wisdom that a soul evaluates what was left incomplete from previous lives, determines what goals will be addressed in the coming life, and scans a variety of possibilities. The details are considered, and there are many options.

Through this process, a soul determines if a particular environment – birth family, type of body, and potentials of the scenario – fit with their life goals.

Do you mean that a Soul chooses which body it is going to come into?

It is not an intellectual choice, such as how a human personality makes decisions. Rather, each soul lands in the situation that suits the growth and balancing needed to move them along the soul evolution process.

Can we change the path we have selected? What part does free will play in all of this?

A particular setup is chosen for anticipated opportunities and results. That path is modified by free will. Even if a soul sets out to complete agreements and interact with soul family members, accidents and the choices others make also have an influence.

There is free will to either embrace or avoid the path selected, to go in a different direction, but there are also results and consequences of every choice. With the awareness between lives a soul would realize, "I was avoiding my goal and now I need to try again."

The wisdom of the soul says, "If I start at this point, my first choices lead to the next choices that lead to these other choices." Every Earth journey has many forks in the road. There is a blending of planned agreements for what your soul will attempt and decisions you make as a human in response to what randomly happens.

How does a soul come into the denseness of a physical body?

A soul in the Spirit realm is like a bright ball of white light. To contain that limitless energy in the physical, there is a pulling in, a focus, like a laser beam.

As a human body develops through nine month of gestation, there is a transition process where the soul experiments with sometimes being in the growing body and sometimes not, in order to accustom their vast energy to a confined space. In order to adapt to the physical, even before birth, a soul blends with the mother's essence: her body, soul, and emotions, to gain an idea of how well their vibrations resonate. Initially, the soul of the baby is present in her body for brief periods, returning to the Spirit realm and the Universal Soul to review and assimilate the feelings and perceptions gained through the mother. As that soul travels back and forth, it becomes more accustomed to the change in frequency between the physical and nonphysical realities.

This transition is like getting into a hot bath. You have

to stick your toe in and out, a little bit at a time, to get used to the drastic change in temperature. With each dip, the water becomes more comfortable and you move in deeper.

How many souls are there?

There are not a finite number of souls. Souls are drawn in from the Spirit realm as needed, in a gradual progression, to accommodate however many human bodies are on the planet. As the population of the Earth grows, the number of souls increases. At any point, some souls have been here many times, while others are new. Like passing through a revolving door, new souls are arriving, while others are returning in the cycle of reincarnation, and old souls are completing their sequence of lives, not returning to Earth.

Whenever there are more physical bodies than there are souls returning to Earth, new groups form up and begin a cycle of lives as baby souls, much like air moving to fill the void created in a vacuum.

Are there male souls and female souls?

The soul itself has no gender. Gender is a condition of the physical body, and part of the polarity of Earth. Some lives are lived as a female, others as a male for a variety of opportunities. For instance, in order to experience childbirth, you must be a woman. In order to feel the physical strength of a male body, you must spend time in one.

Immersed in a particular focus, a soul may incarnate primarily as one gender during a series of lives, but every soul will eventually experience both.

When people speak of male or female energy, it is not a gender designation so much as a description of the direction that energy moves while in a body. Female energy, as an essence, moves inward – the containment of Spirit – a state of being. Male energy, as an essence, moves outward – Spirit expressed in a new form – a state of creating. A male body can embrace female energy, and vice versa. The Earth challenge involves balancing of the male and female energies within either gendered form.

What about animals? Do they have souls?

Humans need to have individualized souls – to grapple with, understand, and come to peace with the physical separation. Animals exist more as a group soul. They are in separate bodies, but share and benefit from the experiences and growth of the whole, without feeling alone in their physical forms as humans do. What happens during life and death are cumulative lessons, being that the awareness gained through an experience by a smaller group influences the mass.

For a domesticated animal such as a cow or goat, their contact and interaction with people adds complexity to the learning. As a pet, the animal is introduced to human emotion, feeling what their human feels. In such close proximity, the animal is allowed an introduction to the human challenge of physical separation and emotional experiences.

Are dolphins and whales different than other animals?

The cetaceans are the exception in the animal kingdom, incarnating as individualized souls. In contrast to humans, they remain aware and connected to Universal Soul (through their soul families) and to *all that is*. Less concerned with the fears, challenges, or lessons of balancing with other souls, their Earth experience involves fully embracing the joy of living as physical beings while retaining their spiritual nature. From one life to the next, not much changes. They are simply being.

Where do souls go once they complete their cycle of lives?

Once a soul has mastered the challenges of living, having accomplished all personal balancing and soul purpose goals, they can choose to come back to Earth in a body, or not. They may return for a few more lives – human, but beyond the human pain and struggle – to be of service to others, and to experience the full joy and empowerment of living.

Eventually, the cycle of coming back into a body is complete and there is reunion with soul family members in the non-physical realm as well as blending with the unlimited essence of Universal Soul.

The next stage of soul development involves remaining in the Spirit realm and interacting with soul family members who *are* still in bodies. As Spirit Guides, these souls are beyond the challenges of Earth, but continue evolving as they assist others who are still in the physical world.

Are there dark energies in the world?

The concepts of good and evil do not exist outside of the physical realm and the human frame of reference. The Spirit realm and Infinite Synergy do not have polarity as a factor. All is simply energy. Benevolent and malevolent, helpful and adverse, are terms assigned to human behavior, not the laws of the Universe. It is only the human perspective that interprets something as good or bad, usually as a response to comfort or fear. There are forces that create and forces that unravel, but these are more an aspect of your own soul, or the influence of another in the soul family (including your Spirit Guides), not some being beyond the human/soul existence. When people speak of dark energies affecting individuals or groups of people, it is really no more than their own human struggle with confusion and pain creating their state of being or behavior.

Are there dark souls, evil souls?

There are no souls who are evil, only souls who are so

disconnected from their soul essence as to exist in a perpetual state of confusion and pain, life after life. Characterized as not learning from their mistakes no matter what they go through and unable to make deep emotional connection with others, they continue with behavior that causes frustration and suffering.

Like a small child abandoned to learn and survive on their own, these souls grapple with getting their needs met any way they can. Instead of gaining true inner strength, they settle for the illusion of power. Instead of authentic bonding, they engage in invasive and controlling relationships. They stay fixed in whatever emotionally charged situation they left behind, becoming trapped in cycles of revenge and power struggles.

For a variety of reasons, they remain lost in their human confusion, without ever remembering or embracing the deeper soul essence.

What happens to these souls? Do they go to Hell?

These souls, though their actions may seem horrible, are serving the greater good in their role of agitator, spurring others to awareness and growth they would not arrive at otherwise. It is a most powerful accomplishment to overcome the challenge of an adversary, to develop and maintain inner strength and emotional compassion when faced with a relentless opponent.

Souls who have such a role face the risk of becoming so far off their own path of growth and development, that they are never able to progress. In that case, or when a soul becomes a deterrent to the soul growth and paths of others, they are drawn back to the source, Spirit and *all that is*. Much like pouring a small cup of poison into a vast unlimited sea, it will not taint the ocean, but the poison will be so dispersed as to no longer exist.

The Hell you refer to, where an evil-doer burns for all eternity, does not exist, nor would it serve any purpose.

So will these dark souls ever come back to Earth?

New souls are always pure. Any soul dissolved into Infinite Synergy returns to a blended state, as they were before they ever started their cycle of lives. They no longer exist as an individualized soul, dark or otherwise.

Do some humans not have a soul?

All human beings have a soul. To be without one would be too confusing and disruptive to the others.

Those who seem to be living without a soul are only so because they have lost touch with their soul essence – a result of emotional trauma, heavy drug abuse, or other adverse influences.

Is it possible for a person's soul to be stolen by another?

No. A person can feel as if they have lost their vitality or sense of self, but it is not possible to take someone's soul essence. People may give over their free will or become so enmeshed with another that they no longer have control of basic choices and appear as mindless as a victim in a vampire movie. "He has lost his soul to the dark energies," only describes someone who has given over to confusion and manipulation.

The soul is still present, just not in charge.

Is there such a thing as soul death? Could a soul be destroyed through intense trauma such as an atomic blast?

Even in the most violent of deaths, only the physical body is disintegrated. The soul lives on. There will be residual effects in the cellular memory - by degrees and circumstance – depending on the manner of death.

When a person dies naturally and gently, they flow through a gradual transition to the nonphysical realm of essence. Being killed in an act of violence disrupts the process of adjusting to being out of the body. Any energy from unresolved traumas at death are brought into the next incarnation to be processed and transmuted.

The residual pattern will be different for a person whose head is chopped off (felt as neck pain) versus a person who dies in a fire (later expressed as rashes or skin pain). Being

---

killed in an explosion, like an atomic blast, leaves the cellular memory of being boiled from the inside, but even that does not annihilate the soul. No matter what destruction is inflicted upon the body, no matter what traumas are emotionally endured, no matter what mistakes are made, the soul lives on.

As a soul in a physical body, while experiencing the challenges of life, keep in mind that this life is just one pearl on the string of pearls. All that is going on around you is part of living, part of the adventure here. Retaining the perspective of soul essence helps you view situations like a movie, rather than getting emotionally embroiled or devastated by events. Though it is easy to get caught up in it, the human drama is only one aspect of your soul's existence.

BETWEEN LIVES

Beyond this human life, your soul lives on.

How long does a soul take between lives?

The cycle of reincarnation is like a revolving door, from the physical to the non-physical, into the physical again. There is no set number of years that it takes between lives, because time doesn't exist beyond the Earth plane, and because the reactions and needs of each soul varies.

A Soul will take as long as is needed to integrate all that was experienced, achieved and learned in a lifetime. Between lives, a soul will gain deeper meaning of events and emotions, understand what was left incomplete, heal traumatic interactions, and then chose and prepare for the next earth adventure. Without this transition, entry into the new life would be like coming home from a challenging battle assignment wounded and weary, and immediately being sent on another mission without recuperation or preparation.

Where does a soul go in between lives?

A soul moves into the realm of Spirit, where there is a reunion with soul family members who are also between lives, like drops of water gathering into a bucket.

Initially, as the soul leaves the body, there is a "holographic" experience that is representative of the frame of reference and belief system of the human personality. If a person believes in judgment and Hell, the still lingering mind may create a pit of fire and punishment. If a person anticipates Angels in Heaven, that is what this initial experience will bring. If a person has no religious notion or sense of an afterlife, floating in a void or looking back on Earth may be the sensory experience. Eventually, the mind disburses, and only the soul essence remains.

After the unique experience immediately following death, there are a series of transition phases that are universal to all souls. Each phase is part of a soul's development in the space between lives and is important to go through before coming into another body.

The Letting Go Phase

The first stage prepares a soul for the idea of leaving the physical. In the simplest of transitions, a soul with total awareness could decide, "I've done enough now. It is my time to go." The soul would leave the body gently, without the pain and suffering of a lengthy illness or the sudden wrenching departure caused by an accident or violent event, but most souls do not have the clarity to let go that easily.

In the natural progression of old age or illness, there is an adjustment phase where the soul vacillates between being in the body and visiting the nonphysical realm. They "stick their toe" in the soul family bucket of water to remember where they are going. There are periods of lucid clarity and attentiveness, alternating with times of extended sleep, unconsciousness, or spacing out – an indication that the soul is not fully in the body, but rather, acclimating to the concept of leaving. As a soul becomes more accustomed to being in the Spirit realm, the thread connecting the soul to the body becomes increasingly thin.

Why is it so hard for people to let go?

During the death transition, there can be resistance to leaving the emotional bonds and responsibilities that bring a sense of belonging, as well as over-attachment to the physical body or material possessions. Souls may hold on due to a sense of unfinished business in their soul tasks or relationship agreements. Others may be afraid of punishment due to their religious beliefs, feel that dying is like giving up, or simply have a fear of the unknown.

What else happens for people in this phase before death?

As the connection between soul and body weakens, the energy that was once used to control a personality or maintain acceptable behavior goes toward maintaining the life force. Any unresolved anger or pain overflows like water leaking out of a cracked cup. One elderly lady, who had seemed to be solid and independent during her adult life, transformed before her family's eyes back into the fearful and insecure girl she had been as a child. She claimed to be missing things and accused people of stealing from her (much as was the case when she'd had to compete with many siblings). As her subconscious memory became stronger than her conscious will, it seemed that she was reliving parts of her past instead of being able to see things as they were in the present.

During this transition, a person may have revelations and emotional shifts, or be able to let go of previous rigidity. One aging man who had fathered with oppressive strictness was compelled to apologize to his children on his deathbed in an effort to undo past hurts. Another man sought to balance previous greed and stinginess by donating money to a charitable cause.

There can also be mysterious communications, like having a heart to heart conversation with a relative in a dream, or receiving a brief but cryptic phone call from a friend, just days before they pass. Those souls are reaching out from the other side to check in with the people they care about before they leave.

During the Letting Go phase, people will tend to pay less attention to material matters than they had previously. Things that had once seemed important, like money, houses, and wills will become more difficult to deal with. On a practical level, material affairs are best put in order before a soul's focus turns to the Spiritual plane.

The Stepping Out Phase

After biological death, the soul is released from the body, expanding beyond the confines of the physical form. There is a shift towards a much faster frequency, often described as "moving towards the light." Not really a direction or a place, more a state of "being," *as* that light, *as* Spirit, *as* Universal Soul.

From this vantage point, there is the ability to look back at the earthly existence to see the body and those left behind, and to react with shock, fear, sadness, relief or joy. Aspects of the mind still function, helping a soul to understand the lingering emotions and to adapt to the transition.

It is possible for some souls to become fixed in the extreme emotions of the death experience or to have resistance to leaving the physical plane. They may find themselves somewhat trapped here as they focus on continuing their

Earthly interactions, lingering as ghosts until they are able to let go and move on.

Most souls are assisted in a smooth transition by members of their soul family. As a source of unconditional love, this welcoming presence lessens any confusion or trauma as souls step out of the physical. You might be welcomed by loved ones who have died before you, be surrounded by your favorite pets, or find yourself wrapped in the wings of an angel. A soul's visual or sensory experience will be unique, based on its personal expectations and frame of reference, whatever is needed to put the soul at ease.

In addition to being soothed, this is also a stage where a soul may reach out to help comfort people left in emotional pain over their death. "Mom came to me in a dream and told me she was okay now." The communication can be more subtle, or bizarre, as with one woman who found her recently deceased husband's wedding ring sitting on her dresser after years of it being lost.

The Cocoon Phase

Also called the Resting Phase, like floating in a cocoon of light, this phase offers a soul a chance to become accustomed to the vastness of just *being*. There is a gradual expansion of the soul energy and a sense of merging, once again, with the Universal Soul.

From a vantage point well beyond the human frame of

reference, and with full awareness of the greater scope of existence, a soul watches the movie of their life to see how well they were able to address their goals. "How well did I embrace my opportunities and challenges? Did I stay on task for my relationship agreements? Did I rise to the occasion when random events threw me a curve?"

Unlike the human personality who might harshly condemn or blindly deny, the soul observes with objective honesty in order to learn and grow. "I see what happened because of what I did. My greed hurt others and kept me from being loved." Or, upon reviewing how they handled a sticky situation, a soul may gain awareness that they did better than originally assumed.

In this process of understanding life's lessons there is support from the soul family, like a team gathered around the viewing, pointing out what is overlooked or incorrectly interpreted with clarity and loving compassion. There is no "other" judging, but rather a soul asking itself, "When I look back and see who I was, do I like what I see?"

The Healing Phase

Things that were endured on the Earth – poverty, violence, loss, oppression – may continue to resonate on deep levels even beyond the physical. There can be screaming wounds of the soul that need to be healed. Much as a mother cradles a crying infant in her arms, petting and comforting, "there,

there," soul family members on the other side gather to sooth a soul with love. No matter what a soul has been or done, in this phase, it is immersed in a light that melts away any anguish, any suffering of the human condition. With the support of Spirit, the soul essence is rinsed clear.

The Planning Phase

With full awareness of all lifetimes' experiences and learning, a soul embraces the next level of soul growth. "What do I need to learn now? What will be my next adventure?"

Through the collective wisdom of the soul family, rather than some kind of discussion group or directing body, souls are guided to a sense of what is best. Perhaps a soul has recently lived a life of wealth and power and now wants to experience the opposite. "Can I be successful without privilege? I'll choose a life of being abandoned and forced to survive on my own." Or, "I kept to myself last time out of fear of being hurt. This time, I don't want to miss out, so I'll challenge myself to connect and be of service to others."

In all soul "assignments," there are two generalized goals – personal growth and soul purpose – taken on as a two-part task. The childhood environment and early challenges provide the means to gain certain skills and qualities. Though often unpleasant, such personal growth is instrumental to the second part, one's work in the world. "This life I choose to help the poor. To do so, I will first need a childhood that teaches me to have understanding of the conditions of poverty. I'll start out deprived and figure out how to rise above it." If this same soul were to be born into a wealthy family, there might be sympathy for the poor, but not the "hands on" experience that makes a person truly empowering of others. If this soul is not able to overcome their own issues regarding lack, their life's goal of helping others will be difficult, if not impossible, to embrace, even with full and conscious awareness of their soul purpose.

Through a series of lives, the soul purpose may have a consistent theme, whereas the personal growth goals will vary by necessity and soul development. During this Planning Phase, a soul will also look into what needs balancing from previous lives as well as what is important to explore as "soul age" appropriate. The details will be worked out in the next phase, the Selection Phase.

The Selection Phase

With an understanding of the general direction a soul is to take, this phase involves selection of the specific scenarios and relationship agreements. Though nothing is guaranteed, a soul is setting up the life *potential* that will provide the greatest *probability* of accomplishing specific tasks.

This is not an intellectual process, since a soul in the space between lives has no conscious mind, but rather, an observation process whereby a soul scans the potential environments on Earth in an effort to discern: "Who are the parents and siblings I will need? What kind of economic status, what culture?"

Picture each person as resonating at a certain color frequency, a blending of soul age and character with human personality. When two people make love, their individual and combined color vibrations emanate like a beacon. The returning soul scans for the parents whose energy is a certain color, then looks deeper to see how they will get along. "What are my prior relationships with these souls? Will they make agreements with me now? What will my life be like with this family?"

In a non-linear time observation of what might be called the future, with a multitude of story lines and possible endings, a soul evaluates the scenario that each presents. "If I choose this family, I will go to grade school in Chicago. Then dad loses his job. We either move to Los Angeles where I meet a soul mate in high school, or stay there, and I won't meet a soul mate until I go away to college."

Prior to birth, a soul may "visit" two or more family possibilities, checking in, sometimes in the body, sometimes not, to see which one *feels* right. There is a complex communication of souls that goes on in a split second as soul agreements are made with the parents, siblings, and other family members.

Sometimes, a soul is so eager to return that they leap as soon as they spot a certain light. When a soul does not thoroughly evaluate their selection, the person can end up struggling to form bonds in families without soul agreements or adjusting to challenges they are not ready for.

Is it the entire soul family who helps a soul make decisions about its next incarnation?

If there are 300 essences that make up a soul family, at any point there may be 200 who are in bodies on the Earth and 100 accessible in the Spirit realm. A soul between lives can feel the support of the entire group, but there are specific souls, perhaps five to ten, who are particularly well suited to assist with evaluation and selection. However, they do not direct, they only provide perspective. Decisions are always made by the individual soul.

The Birth Phase

In the process of returning to the physical form, there are times when the soul is fully in the body of the developing fetus, and times when the soul is in the realm of Spirit, until they become 100% committed to their birth choice.

In some cases, a soul is so comfortable and bonded in love with the mother that their soul spends most of gestation in the mother's womb. Others may be resistant to a mother's painful emotions or stress and move in gradually as they adapt. A few souls are too uncomfortable with being in a weak physical (baby) body that is compromised due to the mother's body, and wait until their own soul can accelerate a healthy change at birth. And there are souls who are so hesitant to take on the difficult challenges of the coming life that they jump in only at the last minute, right at birth.

All agreements between the soul of the baby and the souls of the mother, father, or siblings are tentative, up until the moment of birth. Miscarriages, still births, and accidents are sometimes indications of a change in soul plan, though natural physical problems are also the cause. While in the mother's womb, a baby's body can survive without having the soul present. Once born, it cannot survive without its own life source – the soul.

Is the situation on the other side the same for everyone, even in the case of suicide or murder?

All souls go through a similar sequence of phases, though with variations according to the individual. Some souls breeze through certain phases, while lingering in others. If a soul is too eager to return, they may rush through the Selection Phase. Others, struggling with leaving the physical, may get stuck for a time in the Stepping Out Phase. In the case of those who cause or are subjected to severe life traumas or violent deaths, there may be an extra focus on the Cocoon and Healing Phases.

As for suicide, there are many possible scenarios of that

soul choice and each situation must be evaluated on a case-by-case basis. Perhaps a man ends his life out of desperation; there may be relief from the pain or suffering he thinks he is escaping, but his soul will find itself denied the ability to actualize its chosen life tasks. In this case, there can be immediate regret, as the soul sees how to easily address what the human personality found so difficult.

For some souls, suicide is a means of leaving a life when the person's physical body is not capable of fulfilling the soul's path. Perhaps there is an unforeseen event that causes a woman to have such a severe disability that it would be impossible for her to actualize her soul tasks. Even though there is still the choice to live out the life as is, the soul may chose to try again in another life rather than to endure suffering or dependency on another.

Suicide may also be an exit when a soul's goal is accomplished but natural death is not forthcoming. For a soul with extremely difficult life circumstances such as terminal imprisonment, or severe drug addiction, physical disease, or mental illness, that limitation may be a path to addressing a certain soul lesson or balancing. Once the soul has experienced enough, and the goal is complete, to extend living would do more harm than good by continuing suffering for others or creating additional soul imbalances.

Each situation creates different consequences for the soul. Souls who have ended their human life through suicide may need extra healing and evaluation in the phases between lives to overcome the suffering endured. Or a soul may learn to pay more attention to the Selection Phase for the next life and avoid circumstances that create such overwhelming despair and frustration. If when reviewing their life, a soul learns that their suicide was a human mistake, that there was a different way to solve the Earthly problems, they will probably try something other than suicide in the future. It is all part of the soul learning process.

For people who have murdered, created violence, or caused great suffering for others, their souls will view those actions and have the opportunity to *feel* what their victims endured during the Cocoon Phase in order identify with the effects of their behavior. Those souls will then need the spiritual compassion and understanding that comes through the Healing Phase to clear them of whatever pain or trauma motivated those harmful choices. In the Planning Phase, these souls may establish relationship agreements that will balance the previous violence.

When does life begin? When does life end?

Life of the body, or life of the soul?

A philosophical issue, this question is better rephrased as, "At what point does the soul enter or exit the body?" The answer is complex, and has been addressed earlier in the explanations of the Birth and Stepping Out Phases. Each soul's journey is unique, and it is neither possible nor relevant to establish a rule for all cases.

From the human perspective, life begins and ends according to medically established measurements. For the soul, life exists whether in a body or not.

The cycle of lives is a chain of potential and actualization. When you are on the other side, your soul reclaims full soul essence and wisdom, but only while in the physical form on Earth do you get to play out your intentions.

THE EARTH SUIT

To be part of this world, your soul needs a
physical body.

While on your Earth adventure, your soul needs a way to experience, to move about, to feel, think, and relate to others. The term "Earth Suit" refers to the temporary "costume" your soul "wears" as you *do* all of these things, but it is more than just your body. The Earth Suit is an interactive system for human functioning, a combination of the physical body, the mind, emotions and ego, as well as the less tangible aspects of the energy centers and the soul memories. You are not your human form, though your soul is in one.

Okay, so what's so great about having a body?

When you are in the Spirit realm, you may not have to deal with the challenges of the Earth existence, but you also don't get to feel the warmth of the sun or the satisfaction of being nourished by a delicious meal. You can't rejoice in the exhilaration of running or the sensual pleasure of skin on skin.

The human body (Earth Suit) can be viewed as a tool to experiment with, a way of understanding and interacting with the world around you. What feels good, what doesn't? What keeps you healthy, what doesn't? What makes you thrive, what doesn't? With a body, you are able to evaluate what is happening, to make choices and take action and to interact with others through language, expression and touch.

How would you operate here without it? You would be as a ghost, unable to actualize your intentions.

The human body, with a sense of individuality defined by the ego, gives a person the perspective of "who I am now" as compared to "who I have been" or "who I am becoming." You become aware of how you are growing and changing within your life.

This individuality also gives you the opportunity to sort out your experiences from that of another person, to understand your feelings, thoughts and choices as separate from another. "*I* feel sad, even though people around me are not."

Your physical bodies naturally create a certain distancing between souls that is important for individual focus, but you are not meant to feel alone. The challenge is to maintain a consciousness of shared experience while existing in individual bodies. With your bodies, you relate by seeing and hearing each other, and communicating. You can share love through actions, words or touch. Though not always automatic or simple, there are many opportunities to maintain communion with other souls who are also here doing their individualized experience.

Without a body, you wouldn't be able to move. A tree cannot ask, "Should I go this way or that way?" But you can choose with whom to be connected, or not. In a body, you can say, "This feels good. I will stay here," versus, "This doesn't feel good. I will leave." Your body is the vehicle that sets your choices in motion as you respond to the subtle vibrations received from your environment and other souls.

What do you mean, "responding to vibrations received?"

The pulse of the universe moves as a wave of vibration transferring energy throughout. While in a body, you relate to that movement within a system defined by the physical world. The particular vibration of your soul essence, as well as energy from the environment, other people, and Universal Soul, are modified as those frequencies move through your unique physical structure, emotional energy, and thought patterns.

Each human body is designed to receive these vibrations, interpret these signals as harmonious or disruptive, blend the wave with their own frequency, and broadcast the modified wave out into the world. Picture a person standing at a microphone saying, "Testing." The sound enters the electronic device and is transformed into radio waves. As the signal is relayed, the oscillation alters slightly, though without changing the sound entirely. The word "testing" doesn't become the word "animal" or anything else, but the tonal quality that is projected out of the speaker does not have the exact same resonance as when it first touched the receiver.

How does a body receive these vibrations and what happens in this process you describe?

The soul comes into an Earth Suit, a complex compilation of sensors, processors, and transmitters, and begins receiving and evaluating the frequencies of the Earth environment.

Your eyes catch oscillating rays of light, and you perceive various shapes and colors. A pulsing rhythm of sound is heard as throbbing bass or melodic treble notes, according to the wave pattern reaching your ears. Your skin comes into contact with H_2O, and you feel frozen ice, fluid water, or misty vapors, depending upon the frequency. Your unseen senses pick up the less tangible emanations of love or anger, peace or danger. Like a sponge soaking up water, the cells of the body absorb a pulse of emotions – what other people feel and project blends with your inner responses.

Each of you will receive and respond to these varying

impulses according to the frequency of your physical and emotional bodies. If a person is sad, the energy of their being is vibrating at a decreased rate. Being exposed to faster frequencies of light, sound, or touch will modify the vibration into a higher mode. Exposing an agitated person to slower frequencies helps calm and harmonize their accelerated and perhaps chaotic vibration.

All of the senses work together allowing you to observe and relate to the physical world while the signals are synthesized and translated into information by the mind. The brain itself is another sensor, directly receptive to input that leads to new ideas and insights.

Certain frequencies trigger instinctual reaction to protect us from harm. Some reach the conscious mind as pertinent information. Other vibrations may not be immediately applicable or readily understood, or they may be too uncomfortable to address without shattering the psyche (like child abuse), and so are transferred to the subconscious and stored for later comprehension. When a person has gathered enough other information for the "puzzle" to make sense (and they are mature enough to deal with it), those "missing pieces" are released into the conscious mind, showing up as "aha" moments of clarity and understanding.

All vibrations are moving simultaneously; the actions and reactions play off of each other like ripples coming from opposite ends of a pond. Signals, relays, evaluation, response. The Earth Suit is a multifaceted interpretation center for the soul.

How is all this information processed?

In a complex system of energy centers located throughout the body. These focal points, like little satellite dishes picking up radio waves, are each tuned to specific frequencies and operate as transfer stations, relaying signals to the appropriate aspect of the body. Some of the energy centers described here relate directly to the traditional Chakra system, while others do not. (The Chakra system, originally known in Eastern spiritual traditions, is now commonly recognized in many teachings.)

The energy centers allow your sensory experience to be interactive and unified. These spheres of energy along the spinal axis of the body transfer a particular frequency received to whichever aspect of the earth suit speaks the language. The physical body, the senses, emotions, ego, and mind are each the interpreters. Vibrations are translated into messages pertinent to the functioning of each area.

Your energy centers help you stay connected to the Earth, to Spirit, and to each other. Even though the centers are not physical, they interact with and trigger physical things. Like wind and sun to a leaf, energy centers act upon the body, bringing it to life.

Where are these energy centers and what do they each do?

The Crown Center: (7th – Crown Chakra). Located just above the head, it serves as a point of entry for infusion of Spirit and Universal Soul – pure electro-magnetic energy, love, and wisdom – to flow into all of the other centers. Awareness of this "satellite dish," also allows access to your higher self and Spirit Guides, via messages relayed to the Mind Center.

The Mind Center: (6th – Third Eye Chakra). As a non-physical aspect of the brain, the Mind Center occupies the space inside the skull and is the common link between the conscious, subconscious, and super-conscious functioning. This center allocates vibration to be translated into the mental language of automatic thinking (subconscious), intentional thinking (conscious), and inspired thinking (super-conscious).

The mind center receives vibrations transmitted from the physical body, senses, and emotions, as well as from people, the physical Earth, and the Spirit realm to be processed for understanding. This center is also the source point that sends messages to other centers, activating them to release responses of feelings, words, and actions.

The Vocal Center: (5th – Throat Chakra). This center, encompassing the neck area, functions as the tool for personal self-expression, allowing you to project a wave of emotion, ideas, and intentions to others. More a broadcaster than a receiver, the Vocal Center is the bridge between the mind and the heart, blending your thoughts and emotions into verbal communication. It is your avenue for relating and connecting to others.

The Heart Center: (4th – Heart Chakra). The Heart Center is the receptacle for emotional essence in your being. Like a cup, it holds the frequencies of feelings that are poured in directly or via other energy centers. The heart center picks up vibrations emanating from the body (what you sense physically), the subconscious (what you have felt in the past), the mind (what you think you feel), and the instincts (what you fear), bringing all resonance of those feelings into the present moment.

You can take in the vibration of other people (what someone else feels), as well as the soul family (eternal love and belonging). And, you can emote the essence of what is held in your heart (expressing through a combination of thoughts, words, and actions) for others to absorb. Projecting and receiving emotion is the avenue souls use to stay connected while in the physical separation.

The Power Center: (3rd – Solar Plexus Chakra) Just below the rib cage, in the exact center of your being, the Power Center is the "battery pack" of your Earth Suit. Much as the planet has a source of energy – fire at the center – so does your body. When a soul enters a physical form, there is a vital essence that comes in, a force to sustain the spark of life and to fuel reactions. A pulsing globe of brilliant light, the radiant vibration of your Power Center is as individual as a fingerprint, identifying your unique soul energy. When danger is sensed, instinctual memory reaches the Power Center, instantly relaying a call to action through the nervous system – chemical reactions (adrenaline), automatic muscle movement, and heightened awareness.

The Emotional Storage Center: (2nd – Sacral Chakra). The functions of the Emotional Storage Center correspond with the abdominal area of the body, for the elimination and creation processes. A receptacle for vibrations of accumulated past experience – feelings, life memories, and learned patterns – this center is integrally connected to the subconscious. Sandwiched between the Power and the Root Centers, and resonating with the life-force energy of both, this is where your creative ideas develop and take form. When unpleasant or confusing feelings (yours or someone else's) come in through the heart center, and are not dealt with, their vibration ends up in this center. Whichever frequency is stronger, disturbing emotions or clear creativity, will be what incubates and grows here.

The Root Centers: (1st – Base Chakra). With a focus on survival and sexual drives, the Root Centers serve the interrelated functions of receiving and transmitting vibrations of a primal nature. There are two aspects of the Root Center, the Sex Center (near the front of the pubic bone), and the Earth Root (an invisible extension of your spinal column).

Operating as one, the Root Centers trigger the body's instinctual reactions. When sensing danger, the Root Centers activate DNA soul memory to be released through the system, like a cry of "fire." The message, "previous harm," is sent to the Power Center (activating immediate response), a wave of intense discomfort is relayed to the Heart Center for emotional awareness, and the story is relayed to the Mind Center for evaluation. Individually, the two Root Centers serve specific functions.

The Sex Center is the seed point of sexuality, which fuels the human desire to create more than "what is just me." In the blending of energy or the creation of a new life form, the nature of the souls will determine what is given birth to. Beyond basic drives and procreation, sexual union allows you to merge with another, physically, emotionally, mentally and spiritually, in a dance with the Divine, as an opportunity to revitalize your entire being while emanating a broadcast of love.

The Earth Root grounds you firmly to the physical earth providing a lifeline to the vital essence of the planet. Like having a root growing down from the base of your spine into the center of the earth, you are able to tap into an unlimited source of strength and energy. Much as a tree without roots, the physical body has difficulty surviving without this lifeline.

How do our energy centers work together as a system?

In any situation, your energy center system receives input, interprets it and then responds. Here's what happens:

A person standing near you says, "I don't like that color green on you."

Your ears receive the vibration of tones in each syllable and your brain translates those signals to words that can be consciously understood. Simultaneously, your eyes pick up the images of facial expression and gestures – body language – also sent to the brain for interpretation and meaning. Your brain interprets a frowning mouth and down-turned eyebrows to mean hostility – an association let's say, from a memory when someone with a similar look hit you.

A vibration of deep emotional pain emanates from the person speaking, like smoke pouring out the window of a burning building. The frequency of pain is received by your energy center "satellite dishes," creating a resonant "Boing!" The word patterns hit your Mind Center and your brain takes in a thought/belief to be analyzed as true or false. Raw emotion hits your Heart Center to register feeling – yours and theirs – in the present time moment. The intensity of vibration goes straight to your Power Center (solar plexus) to be interpreted as "safe or not safe." A pulse of disturbance – distorted energy rather than pure Spirit – shoots from your Power Center into the cells of your physical body as if taking in a poison tincture. Your energy center's system of invisible messengers relays the vibrations from each receptor point to where they need to go for evaluation and response.

Your brain sends the translated message "you are disliked" to your Mind Center, (to be interpreted by both the conscious and subconscious aspects). Sensing non-acceptance, your Heart Center sends the translation, "when you wear green, you are disliked," to be logged into your Emotional Storage Center for future reference. Your Power Center, resonating "Danger! Avoid pain!" activates responses in your physical body – tension, adrenaline. Without thinking, you react with the retaliation of defensive words or aggression, the safety of silence or retreat, or the cry for nurturing that comes with tears (depending on what has worked in the past).

The taking in and transference of raw data happens in a split second, while your conscious mind attempts to evaluate the signal as relevant or not. How often have you thought of a more appropriate response some time later or dwelt on the words and feelings of a disturbing conversation long after it was over? Before you can think clearly, the message is transferred for automatic response and lodged into your subconscious. Your conscious mind becomes even less effective when clouded with irrational thinking or out of control emotions.

Depending on your system's attunement, or resistance, to the frequency sent, the simplified message, "I don't like you," will be accepted or rejected, with a correlating response of words, actions, and feelings. If you are accustomed to receiving criticism or the emotional projection of another's pain – not because you like to, but just out of familiarity – this message, matching the vibration of what you are already holding in your being, slides in like Cinderella's foot to the glass slipper.

Your subconscious, having stored learned associations from past trauma, warns, "I remember being hurt when I was disliked." The details of the event – either from childhood or a past life - are not immediately accessed or reevaluated until your conscious mind asks, "What is the same? What is different than before? Is there really a danger? What is the best response now?"

Your conscious mind gathers all input, including refuting information, and makes a new assessment. "This situation, this person, is different than the past. I am not going to be hurt or abandoned if I am criticized. I am safe, even if I do not agree."

New signals from your Mind Center are transmitted through the system for response. "I am safe," is the message sent to your Power Center, resonating with a sense of comfort rather than threat, relaxing instinctual responses. "I am not abandoned. I am okay," is the message sent to your Heart Center, presenting a calm feeling rather than rejection. Instead of a fearful response, the expression from your Mind and Vocal Centers can now be one of neutral acknowledgement and engagement, "I am sorry that you don't like green. What color do you like better?"

What you feel inside, and how the other person responds, sets off the next wave of vibrations to be assimilated through the same process – input, evaluation, and reaction. As you experiment with receiving and interpreting signals through this system, you learn what is healthy for you and what is not.

All is vibration - perception, emotion, sensation – and it all goes in. Like a sponge soaking up a dirty spill, your being holds painful emotions and soul memories. Even without your awareness, ignored feelings will still resonate, and all frequencies will be broadcast through the system. The stronger the vibration, the louder the volume.

Isn't there any way for a person to control what is broadcast through the system?

As you learn and grow, you naturally develop the ability to shut out the frequencies that don't feel good. Your aura, as a sensing shield, becomes tuned to uncomfortable vibrations. When you enjoy the feelings that come in, your aura expands to take in a greater area of awareness. When danger or painful feelings are detected, your aura retracts, containing and shielding like a tight suit of armor.

What is an aura?

An extension of the physical body, the aura defines the sphere of influence of the soul essence. Much like an invisible outer skin, this energy field functions as an auxiliary sensor and filter system. The aura is a receiver that allows you to sense subtle energies outside of your body, and a projector which extends the range that your personal vibrations can be broadcast beyond your physical form.

As you gain awareness of your auric field, you can take charge of what is allowed in, what is expressed out, and how much space your energy is filling. This skill enhances your ability to be sensitive and open, or not, depending upon the situation.

How does a person control what comes in through the aura?

You can learn to use your aura as a shield, as if it were an opalescent bubble that you walk around in. By imagining such a force field around you, all that is light and feels good can easily move through, but anything that would be uncomfortable will bounce off.

To be more in control of what comes into your being from specific people, you need awareness of the unseen energy cords that are formed between each other's energy centers.

What are energy cords?

Energy cords form the lifelines to other souls with whom you have come into contact in your life. They are the links that maintain the unlimited blending that your soul feels while in the Spirit realm. With earthly bodies you talk to each other and touch each other, but you also create subtle connections, on a soul level, without conscious awareness. Like telephone lines, invisible cords transfer messages between people. Vibrations of an emotional nature are dialed in at the Heart Center, while frequencies of a mental nature are relayed through cords at the Mind Center, and those of a sexual nature move through Sex Center cords.

Are cords always present? What determines the connection?

Energy cords are temporary bonds of the physical world, created through the natural desire to feel soul community as you would in the Spirit realm. Though you may have intention on a soul level, until you come into contact with a person you don't have any cords with them.

Like dialing a telephone number, a cord between Mind Centers is hooked up to have a meeting of the minds, to better understand each other. This is what is happening when, during a conversation with a friend, you both come up with the same idea or phrase at exactly the same instant. Heart Center cords deepen and maintain intimate emotional relationships, especially during times of physical separation, as when a mother has a sense that something is wrong while her child is at school.

Are cords maintained throughout an entire lifetime?

Each situation is unique. How long you maintain a cord is a matter of preference and awareness. For connections with soul family members agreeing to help with ongoing love and support through difficult challenges, the cord may be lifelong.

Cords between soul family members are formed and maintained as you help each other. In the gentlest of agreements, a cord is formed to send additional love and support as a person goes through difficult challenges. To share a connection with a soul with whom you are familiar, having shared other lifetimes in an enjoyable way, may be of additional comfort. Upon meeting the person in this life, there is an unconscious connection, as you say, "Oh, yes, I remember it felt good to be connected to you before. Let's do that again."

When there is a soul agreement to accomplish a certain

task together, especially an uncomfortable or adversarial one, energy cords provide an extra bond to hold you together so that you don't avoid the lesson. Once the task is complete, the temporary cord does not serve a purpose. You can reevaluate the exchange and say, "Thank you for toughening me up. We can now release the cord that bound us together."

How does a person know who they are connected to?

The energy cords are extensions of your sensory system, allowing for perception beyond sight, sound, and touch – almost like antennae. Just as you learn to pay attention to your body, mind and emotions, you can become aware of subtle energies transmitted through these cords to discern what is being received and discover their source. "Am *I* actually feeling sad or am I taking in *someone else's* loneliness?" "Am I clear in *my* mind or am I interpreting the thoughts of another?" "This panic doesn't seem like *me*. Whose fear am I reacting to?"

What about energy cords that bring pain?

Many energy cords enhance our connections, such as when we have an intimate relationship that feels good, and we desire to keep the love flowing on a continual basis. Others cords cause problems, as when you have had an intense argument with someone and afterwards don't seem to be able to shake the sense of continuing conflict. Without realizing it, a cord is transferring hostile energy long after you needed it to interact.

When you make a cord with someone who resides in emotional pain, and your feelings are blended, you can become confused about what is causing their pain and begin to believe that you are responsible for their feelings. An example is a baby, seeking unconditional love and belonging. "I want to feel connected. I'll hook into Mom." But Mom is stressed and angry. The mother's pain comes through the connection, instead of the love that is sought.

What do you do when someone you love is in pain, and you still want to connect with them?

Focusing on sending love and not expecting to receive it, like imagining the one-way flow of water in a hose, projects the good feelings they need without allowing their pain to flow back to you through the heart cord. It will not alleviate their hurt to allow their suffering to flow into you.

Be aware when you are trying to feel close with a person who has shut their heart off out of fear of pain. Their resistance to feeling what you feel interferes with their ability to form a heart cord, to exchange emotion or receive love. So no matter how much love you send to them, not only do they not feel it, but they are not capable of sending it back.

So how do we monitor what goes in and out through these cords?

Like deciding to hang up on a disturbing telephone conversation, you can choose to disconnect the cords that no longer serve you. Or you can clear the line of static, filtering out the pain that interferes with love and support or heightened understanding.

You can imagine that the cords between you, at your heart and head, are filtered much like a mud screen in a garden hose. The clear water flows, the love flows, but the debris doesn't make it to the flowers. In this way, you learn to filter the other person's disturbing emotions without feeling separate.

Monitoring what goes in and out through energy cords is an extension of creating healthy boundaries. Just as you learn to not allow someone to hit you or say terrible things to you, you can make choices about the types of vibration that you are open to receiving.

Being able to identify and control what is happening in your body, both in the physical form and subtle energies, is part of learning to live well here. Like a car you travel around in, your Earth Suit can take you where you want to go. The journey can be difficult or pleasant, dependent upon how well you are taking care of what you are riding in.

SOUL MEMORIES

Your Earth Suit holds the key to your past.

There is an imprinting of vibrations carried over from other times, messages from the soul to the new body so that old traumas and lessons can be remembered instead of repeated.

Where are the soul memories?

The soul memories are in the body's DNA – intricately detailed and complete. More than just a genetic code for the physical form, DNA is the code for the soul consciousness, holding a record of everything that has happened to a soul in any other lifetime, in any other body.

The DNA stores the past life vibration, until there is a reason for the memory to come to awareness in this life. When a similar scenario presents itself, the DNA code is activated (like turning on a light switch) and the message is circulated through the Earth Suit system.

What kinds of codes are held in the DNA?

Some codes relate to previous physical bodies, keeping you from repeating life-threatening dangers. Falling off a cliff in one life produces the instinctual survival response of backing away from the edge of high places. Other codes record emotional traumas. Feeling uncomfortable helps you avoid making choices that have caused trouble in the past. Intellectual knowledge is held in the DNA – you are not relearning everything from one life to another, so much as you are remembering.

There are physical predisposition codes as well. Unlike a gene transferred from a parent determining a genetic trait, in the case of diabetes, this cellular fingerprint does not manifest as the actual disease of diabetes. Instead, the physical body in this life will have a sort of shadow, or residual, manifestation. More like a scar than an actual wound, the predisposition is slight or temporary, perhaps showing up as hypoglycemia or problems with circulation in the legs. When there is a purpose for the person to recall what the soul had previously learned, the body screams, "Hey! Remember when you had diabetes?"

Painful emotions and coping skills developed in one life can carry into another, predisposing you to repeat patterns based on familiarity rather than what serves you now. A child raised by an abusive parent in a past life may react as a powerless victim when encountering that soul again, even though their relationship roles are different now. Emotional predispositions are much like the areas in a dike weakened by a previous storm, continuing to be the place where the water leaks through. As a warning call for change, the soul shouts, "Remember what happened last time? Don't let it happen again!"

DNA also holds intellectual and creative predispositions, as a store of talents in music, art, science, or language. A child prodigy mastering the violin by age five, a fourth grader understanding complex physics formulas with knowledge beyond their teacher's, a person who quickly acquires a second or third language as if it were their first. When it suits their current life goals and challenges, these predispositions allow souls to pick up where they left off rather than having to totally relearn what they have already mastered.

What makes these encoded predispositions manifest, or not?

For a predisposition to become real in the current life, the wiring needs to be hooked up, and accessed (the light switch turned on).

DNA transferred genetically from parents shows up as physical characteristics in the body because all of the wiring from the DNA to the body is already connected. With soul memory DNA, the predisposition is there, but the wires are loose. At the moment the predisposition is activated by a trigger (something similar or reminiscent of a past scenario), soul memories are released from the DNA, like carrier pigeons launched into the air. As the message of the DNA reaches the receivers of the energy centers and the physical body, the pathways (and wiring) become hooked up.

How do soul memories affect us once triggered?

When a message is sent from the DNA – memory vibration delivered into present time – your being may feel and respond as if the situation which is being triggered is happening for real now, without awareness of the soul memory source. If you have been poisoned in a past life, being forced to drink vile-tasting medicine in this life may trigger that soul memory, possibly manifesting as an actual allergic reaction in your body.

If you have the capacity to understand and assimilate what is coming up, the soul memory message is sent to the conscious mind for analysis and refined action. If not, your system reacts with an automatic response based solely on previous learning, and the trigger only reinforces old patterns. In the case of this example, you might then be even more resistant to taking medicine or fear being poisoned.

With awareness of soul memories and predispositions, you can make a conscious decision about releasing or continuing that pattern – to keep the wiring hooked up, or not. Is your unhealthy body trying to tell you something? Does it still serve you to succumb to an overpowering person? Do you have a gift to reclaim?

All soul memories will be stored in the subconscious until changed by new experience and imprinting. The subconscious is the gateway between the DNA and the rest of the Earth Suit system.

Why is information stored away in the subconscious? Wouldn't it be better to have total awareness?

The subconscious, the automatic thinking aspect of your mind, stores the experiences that are too traumatic to be processed or understood. It is the system operating behind the scenes, providing immediate access to previous experience, and helping you avoid dangers automatically. If in a past life, or childhood accident, you nearly drowned when you fell into water, your subconscious (and the stored fear response) will serve to keep you safe without thinking. But, there are also memories stored in the subconscious that are not really useful. To have them all fully present in your conscious awareness would be overwhelming, like having a hundred movies playing simultaneously in your head.

Are all past life memories stored in the subconscious?

All past life memory sits in the DNA of the body, with no affect on a person until triggered. The subconscious –

totally clear at the beginning of a life – becomes the receiver/storage center for the memories that are activated and released from the DNA. Only when a past life scenario is important to your present life will those memories be sent from the DNA to your subconscious. Like having a whole closet full of clothes, you do not wear them all at once, only what you need each day.

What kinds of things trigger past life memories?

When a similar scenario presents itself, you may have a sense of familiarity or "déjà vu," even if the message is no longer relevant or understood consciously. Having a past life memory triggered can feel like reading something in a language you don't fully understand.

Events and environmental situations that bear a resemblance to past life experiences bring prior learning into present time. Perhaps you experience a gut wrenching nausea, and a fear of isolation and treachery, when faced with the prospect of boarding a ship. Your body is reacting to a soul message, a reminder of a time when, perhaps, you were a ruthless pirate, operating from pure greed and lust. You learned then what it was like to avoid cooperation and cause great suffering. Even without conscious awareness, our present time reaction to the trigger of boarding a ship is designed to keep you from repeating the mistake.

Activities such as sports or hobbies can reconnect you to

a previous time. Riding a horse (the trigger) may bring back a feeling of power and glory, even though you are not aware of your previous life as a Mongol warrior. Taking a weaving class may awaken dormant sensations from a life as a Navajo woman, with the immediate response of either an affinity or aversion to the activity.

Ordinary objects or animals may activate a past life story. If you had been tarred and feathered in a life for speaking out against the politics of the time, you may experience fear and revulsion at your first sighting of a feather in this life. There may also be an association – you hold your tongue and do not speak your opinions – after that fear is triggered.

When you come into contact with a soul from a past life, the resonance of their soul essence can bring back the story of your previous encounter. Whatever the flavor of the relationship in the other life, pleasant or uncomfortable, will be the frequency that is received by your subconscious, then into your emotional, physical, and energetic bodies. Like an old tune being played back to you, you will have a response similar to the time shared before. If that soul had caused you harm or trauma, you may react to their presence with an instant feeling that you need to get away. If they were loving and supportive in the past connection, you may feel an easy comfort and attraction.

Feelings of harmony or repulsion are triggered by

sounds, tastes, and smells that take you back in time. Having lived an enjoyable life as a dairy farmer in the Netherlands, your experience while eating cheese in this life is particularly pleasant and comforting. A person who was tortured as a servant in Asia may have a very strong adverse reaction to hearing Chinese music now.

People are often attracted or adverse to certain styles of dress, home décor, music, hobbies, and cuisine in alignment with their previous associations in either pleasant or difficult lives. With any kind of trigger, the person experiences a blending of vibrations between soul memory and present reality.

Why don't we remember what has gone before once we are born?

It is a case of too much information. To remember everything from all of your previous lives would be too distracting and overwhelming, like having multiple personalities. And, not all experiences are important or relevant.

To illustrate: One life, two souls come in as mother and child. The child acts like a child. The mother acts like a mother. The next life they switch, to have a different perspective and balance. Without a fresh start – forgetting – they could get stuck identifying with the previous role, with the mother acting like a child, or the child acting like the mother.

There is a balance between being totally immersed in the experience of who you are and what you are seeking to learn, and having access to past life information that helps you do that better.

What would be a reason to remember a specific past life?

Remembering who you have been in other times brings meaning to the present life, with insight into why you feel and act the way you do. Not remembering anything that went before the current life, or even that there was a before, is like trying to have a sense of who you are without remembering the first twenty years of your life.

When there is confusion in your life, ask yourself, "Is there another story that could help me to understand what is happening now?" When you are feeling stuck in an old pattern that does not serve you, clarity about the past life experience you are reacting to can help you let go and move on.

An example: Every time you get near a leadership role, you get an overwhelming fear that something terrible will happen. In a past life, you and all of your family were killed because you did not heed a warning as the chief of your tribe. Memory of that life brings insight to your reactions, what lessons to retain, and what associations to let go of. Instead of the false belief that leadership will lead to trauma, remember what you were meant to learn – to lead well by listening to the wisdom of others.

Perhaps there is a person who had killed you in a past life. Without knowing why, when you meet that soul now as a coworker, you are fearful and anticipate conflict, which interferes with your ability to get along in your job. Even though the feeling is strong, there is no real threat this life. By comparison, you gain the tools to release resentment and fear, realizing "this person is not going to kill me this time." You can then turn to look at what your current soul agreement may be, perhaps working together and supporting each other's goals, instead of getting trapped in old responses of retaliation or avoidance.

In close relationships, there is a tendency to step into the familiar role of a past life, rather than address a new interaction. A person can get overly attached or expect a person to act a certain way just because that is how the relationship between the two souls was in a past life. By recognizing and shifting the automatic patterns, you gain the tools to achieve balance on a soul level, and more effective and harmonious actions on a human level.

What is the difference between input from a past life and what is happening now?

All input – current situations and triggered past life memories – floods the system with vibrations.

The main difference is that you have conscious memories

of events in *this* life, giving you a head-start when evaluating the situation. You understand that you don't like horses because one kicked you when you were ten, but you are confused by your fear of dogs (associated with being attacked by wolves in a *past* life).

How do you know if you are reacting to the present situation or a past life?

You are probably reacting to both. To illustrate, let's look at an earlier example. A person says, "I don't like that color green on you." You are now faced with a combination of new experience, childhood memory and past life association.

The words come to you with a charge of emotion *projected* by the speaker. The vibration of *their* present-time agitation is absorbed into your system. The speaker's tone of voice resonates with *your memory* of similar criticism from childhood. In your subconscious, earlier emotional responses of sensitivity and fear are activated, adding to the intensity of what you currently feel and reinforcing your earlier learning.

The speaker's *essence* also triggers a past life association – a faraway time when that same soul accused you of doing something against tribal custom and had you banished. Your soul recognizes the speaker's frequency, remembers the lesson, and a chain reaction of instinctual fear is set off. It is as if someone has turned up your receiver's amplification.

The intensity of sensation is exaggerated, making their words *feel* life threatening, which may cause you to overreact with anger, silence, or running away.

All vibrations resonate through the system: the mind, emotions, body and energy centers. Your Mind Center receives signals from subconscious memory, the belief from childhood, "you are disliked," and from a previous life, "you are about to be banished." Your Heart Center feels the agony of emotional separation. Your physical body responds with a quickened pulse and adrenaline surges.

Fortunately, the rational mind compares the old voices that scream, "Avoid pain!" with more recent and pertinent facts. As childhood and past life memories are brought to conscious awareness, what is no longer meaningful can be reevaluated. "This situation is different. This person has no power over me. I am safe."

New truths, held in the mind, broadcast a wave of revised signals to the body, emotions, and energy center receivers for appropriate action. Vibrations of calm and safety override the original warning message as the more relevant story becomes stronger than the past memories.

Instead of challenging the person's dislike of green, or saying something defensive and confrontational like, "Well you look ugly in blue!" you can respond with the intentional choice of objective neutrality rather than from past fears and associations: "*Why* don't you like green?"

As healthier responses erode the old patterns, new messages are transmitted and recorded in the subconscious and DNA for future reference.

Is information about our past lives anywhere else besides the DNA?

DNA holds the past life memories of one particular soul, an ever evolving map charting out the course of its cycle of lives. The Akashic Record, also called the collective unconscious, is a universal memory of all things that have ever happened to any soul, anywhere, in any time. Much like a library holding knowledge, it is a vast source of information. Access to the wisdom of the Akashic Record can be gained through dreams, visions, past life regressions, or the assistance of a clairvoyant, as can information about one's own soul story.

Soul memory awareness is not intended to further your suffering or hold you in unhealthy patterns. It is a wake-up call from your soul. You are being offered clues and opportunities to take a step out of your past.

THINKING AND FEELING

The mind and emotions are the power tools of
your life.

The human mind has three filters – the subconscious,
conscious, and super-conscious – working together to make
sense of the soul's journey. The frequencies of present time
communication, perception and reasoning are received and
assimilated by the conscious. Vibrations telling the stories
of past experience resonate to and from the subconscious
mind filter. The super-conscious receives frequencies other
than those of the physical realm.

What is the function of the super-conscious?

The super-conscious is the thinking mode of creativity,
intuition, exalted states and brilliant intellect, all of the ways
you can use your mind beyond the mundane, practical, or
logical thinking. Your capacity to receive visions and insights,
to tap into wisdom from beyond your own experience, is

sourced in the super-conscious.

Your super-conscious is the tool you use to bring stored subconscious memories to conscious awareness. It is your gateway to Spirit, functioning as a telephone line connecting you to Spirit Guides and Universal Soul. This aspect of your mind is also an avenue to link you, psychically, with other people, whether you are aware of that connection or not.

How do we use the super-conscious? Is it something we do intentionally, or are there triggers that activate it?

Access can be intentionally sought, while at other times, insight comes through spontaneously. In meditation, visioning, or prayer, the super-conscious works as the receiver for messages from Spirit Guides or your higher soul essence as a means to get clues about the choices you are making.

Dreams can be the subconscious processing of traumas that need to be cleared (recent experiences or symbolic representations of childhood incidents), or simply information being received through the super-conscious. A story of a past life playing like a movie in the dream (complete with real sensations and feelings) may show you what not to repeat, or give you a view of the soul purpose path you are here to be on.

When there is a need, through dreams or while awake, your super-conscious can receive clues of higher knowing about situations or people, giving you direction for events yet to come. In dreams, the logical mind is at rest and does not interfere with or edit the messages that come through from the subconscious or the super-conscious.

No matter what activates the super-conscious, all information is assimilated and interpretted through the brain's mental capacity for conscious understanding.

Wouldn't it be better to operate from the super-conscious, instead of the subconscious?

All three aspects of the mind are important. To operate through only one is too limiting. The super-conscious can bring sublime experiences, reminding a soul of blended existence and bringing through insights and inspirations. There may be a desire to escape the heavier aspects of the human condition, like emotional pain and suffering, by focusing the mind on the super-conscious. Without the conscious mind, you would have a difficult time relating to your physical world or assimilating information in a logical, practical way. Without the stored knowledge of the subconscious, you would be as one who was doing everything for the first time, all of the time.

What about our subconscious, conscious, and super-conscious in regard to when we are first born? Does one become stronger as we develop?

When your soul first comes into the body, your conscious

mind is a minimal aspect of your being. The super-conscious keeps you connected to the unconditional love and wisdom of the Spirit realm, while the subconscious is busy accumulating data relating to your new environment.

You begin to use hearing and sight, but most input is received by the sensing of subtle vibrations, picking up people's feelings and thoughts through the wide-open channels of the Crown, Mind, and Heart Centers.

Much of what you first experience is too confusing for the undeveloped conscious mind to analyze, so the intense emotions of other people or traumatic situations are sent to the subconscious, like storing extra food in a baggie for later. The subconscious is also receiving messages from the DNA as similar childhood experiences activate those stories. "You may need to remember this past life learning."

In middle childhood, your conscious mind begins to limit input through the super-conscious. The degree to which you experience feeling another's pain will effect how much you close down that filter. At the same time, you are utilizing language to communicate with your parents, siblings, and friends so you don't need to rely on relating through subtle sensing alone. As you enter school and expand your intellect, connecting through the conscious becomes the focus. "I am paying attention to right now, and I can figure this out for myself."

You rely less on the learned memories stored in the subconscious and begin to understand some of the confusing experiences and feelings. "What works for me and what doesn't? What is valuable enough learning to carry with me? What can I leave behind?" In the adolescent and young adult phase, there is an emphasis on subconscious processing, in tandem with emotional development.

At the adult stage, it is tempting to think: "This conscious mind of mine works so well, that I can ignore my emotionally confusing past and any intangible dreams or imagination." But shutting out the non-analytical mind functions, the super-conscious and subconscious, is like trying to get somewhere by swinging your arms but not moving your legs.

If you can integrate all three aspects of the mind, old patterns and confusing fears can be analyzed and transformed at the time they are triggered instead of being stored in the subconscious. When memories remain unprocessed by the conscious and super-conscious, they do not go away, but come screaming through the backdoor of your emotions and responses.

At the end of your adult life, the ideal is for you to have cleared enough of your subconscious to have little emotional baggage left, to have let go of emphasis on the intellectual functioning, and to restore your connection with the non-physical realms. As you move toward transition out of the physical body, your super-conscious filter reopens to help you embrace an expanded awareness of what is on the other side. This aspect of your mind creates experiences of blending with the soul family in the Spirit realm that are intended to remind your soul that death is not the end and to help you let go gently.

During the transition phase before death, there is a shift to mostly super-conscious functioning, and those elders may exhibit memory loss, dementia, and even coma. Their conscious mind begins to let go and is no longer the pilot driving the ship. With diminishing mental capacity, there is less ability to process or control emotions. Unresolved emotions can resurface and cause intense and irrational behaviors that seem immature or out of character. The elder transition phase of life is often a return to the baby-state-of-being leaving one wide open psychically, with the super-conscious mind strong, the reasoning mind less active, and the subconscious (hopefully) clear.

How do the three filters of the brain (subconscious, conscious and super-conscious) relate to the Mind Center or the Crown Center?

The Mind and Crown Centers relay vibration to the subconscious, conscious, or super-conscious filter of the brain to be translated into information depending upon which of these filters will be able to interpret the message.

The Crown Center is the satellite dish receiver of frequencies from beyond the physical realm. The super-conscious is the filter that translates information of *that* nature to the conscious mind for mental understanding.

The conscious mind processes all information of an intellectual nature through reasoning and analysis. The subconscious stores memories (of an intellectual or emotional nature) and is one of many sources of messages for the conscious mind to interpret.

The Mind Center receives information from other people in the form of direct communication, as well as thoughts generated internally, to be processed in a conscious way. The subconscious releases triggered memories, the Heart Center sends feelings, the body sends sensory signals, all through the Mind Center, to be translated and understood intellectually by the conscious mind.

I am also unclear about the relationship and interaction of the Heart Center, the emotions, the subconscious and the Emotional Storage Center.

The Heart Center, the subconscious, and the Emotional Storage Center are interactive. The Heart Center receives vibrations of an emotional nature transmitting feelings to the mind, the body, the ego, and the instincts. There are times when it is useful to have automatic thinking and instant response to feelings.

The subconscious receives and translates emotional experiences into associations (I feel unloved when I am criticized). The Emotional Storage Center holds the overflow of painful feelings, giving you a way to temporarily move excess emotion from the Mind and Heart Centers.

When your buttons get pushed (someone speaks critically), the Emotional Storage Center sends vibrations back to the Heart Center (I feel unloved) and/or the subconscious mind (criticism means I am unloved). When there is too much baggage left unresolved in the Emotional Storage Center, past feelings will interfere with clear functioning.

What does it mean to have emotions?

Emotion is the quality of sensing an essence of energy within you, feeling a quality besides the physical body. Serving as the bridge between the physical and the intellectual, emotion is the tool to help you process your experiences and interactions. You pay attention and learn best from situations that bring intense feelings such as fear, anger, grief or love. Your emotions guide you away from suffering and towards joyful experiences.

Through your emotions, you are able to feel what others feel which enables you to have stronger connections than you could have otherwise. Emotions compel you to express the truth of your being, and offer you the ability to experience, on profound levels, what it is to be alive in this world.

Aren't we here to release emotion?

Not all emotion is undesirable. Why would you want to release love, joy, accomplishment or satisfaction? It is only important to let go of the unhealthy or unnecessary emotions.

Previous emotional states can carry over into present time causing pain and suffering; so, part of the task in any given lifetime is to reevaluate and release the patterns that are no longer relevant. The goal is to retain the growth and learning of your experiences, while freeing the traumatic feelings that can enslave you.

Emotion in general is not something to get rid of. The ability to feel is a blessing, not a curse. Life is meant to be a rich adventure, not just a chore to be tackled so that you don't have to be here anymore.

What is the role of the ego?

To have an ego is to have a sense of self, like a tuning fork resonating inside you with a vibration of "I am." Ego individuality creates the ability to differentiate your feelings, thoughts, and experiences from someone else's, to be able to evaluate your personal choices and consequences in a simpler fashion than if you were to remain totally blended with other souls.

Ego is also the aspect that plugs you into the physical body, and calls you to action. In the Spirit realm, there is no separation between souls and no needs to be met. In the physical realm, pure "being" shifts to "doing," and from "we are" to "I am."

Shouldn't we try to eliminate our Ego?

The ego is neither bad nor good, nor something to get rid of, but an aspect of the Earth Suit integral to having an individual physical experience. Without your ego, your sense of self, you would have no strength, no will, and no life. The idea behind "getting rid of your ego" is to not let personal gratification or attachments keep you from working in co-creation with others and to not allow your will or fears to drive your actions. The ego only becomes a problem when the sense of self is out of balance.

A balanced ego brings the ability to embrace the truth of your being – you are essentially the same as Spirit. You have the ability to contain, within your physical body, the essence of love and light in its purest form. You need a healthy ego in order to grasp your greatness, to understand and embrace it, and to achieve your full potential.

Greatness is not about a comparison to another – "I am better than you." Accepting your own magnificence is about believing and feeling the Divine within your own being, and to simultaneously see the Divine in each and every one else. There is nothing wrong with being great.

How do the ego and the emotions interact? Does one control the other?

Emotion asks, "What is the feeling?" Ego reacts to discomfort, "I feel bad," with an impulse to change the feeling.

The ego helps to identify, "How do *I* feel?" rather than "There is a feeling" which may be easily confused with how somebody else feels.

The ego is the voice of the emotions, especially when the soul does not feel good in the body. When there are emotions of love and harmonious connection, the ego is quiet. When you have painful feelings like, grief, loss, or emotional confusion, the ego screams, "Me, me, me! What about me?"

The emotion brings a way of evaluating comfortable versus uncomfortable. The ego gives the motivation to do something about that feeling. Emotion says, "I feel alone" because my love has left me. The ego commands, "Do something! Make this feeling go away!" Reacting to physical requirements like hunger and cold, and also the emotions of fear or pain, the voice of ego says, "I am in danger! Make it safe!" The ego demands a change. *How* you change is driven by your emotions, beliefs and behavior patterns.

Emotion, as a sensory measure of personal experience, asks the question, "What does it feel like to be in the situation I am in right now?" Ego instantly provides the answer, "I am safe," or "I am not safe," and shouts for action.

Is our ego present at birth or developed at some later point?

From the moment your Soul commits to being fully present in the physical body the ego exists and begins to individualize information taken in through the senses. Initially, a soul retains full connection to *all that is*, but with time and experience, the ego becomes more sensitive and developed.

When do we begin to have emotions? When we are in the womb, when we are born, or as we develop in childhood?

Even before birth, vibrations of emotion are received. From the time the Soul connects with the baby body in the womb, there is a blending with the mother through the emotions which allows the soul in the fetus to feel what the mother feels. If the mother is stressed, the baby feels stressed. If the mother is scared, the baby is scared. If the mother is happy, the baby is happy. The unborn soul doesn't have the ego development to process an emotion unique unto itself.

Once born, the ego triggers the emotional experience to become individualized and unique. The ego says, "Here I am!" The emotion now asks, "How do *I* feel?" instead of "How do *we* feel." The ability to interpret emotions develops gradually after birth and throughout the life.

Does emotion come from the heart?

The heart, attracting and processing vibrations of an emotional nature, is not the source. The strongest sensations of joyous expansion or contracting pain may be felt in your heart, but waves related to emotion flow through your entire being.

If you are in a situation of danger, there is a vibration of fear in your solar plexus and belly. You feel it in your gut, with adrenaline kicking in. Deep grief and sadness is often felt both in the heart and in the pit of your belly – the lovesick syndrome – making it hard to eat. During times of excitement or exuberance, looking forward to a pleasant event, energy registers as a bubbling forth expansion in the heart as well as the head.

Imagine that one's heart is like a cup that is designed to receive emotion. The heart holds what you are feeling at the moment. If you fill the heart with hurtful emotions from a week or two ago, by dwelling on events in your mind, the sadness continues to be your present time experience even though events that created the emotion happened a long time ago. No matter what vibrations of love may be coming in, if your mind keeps your Heart Center filled with thoughts of loneliness, loneliness will be your present emotion.

Even though emotions are non-physical aspects of your

being, the health of the heart organ can be beneficially or adversely affected by the vibrations resonating there.

So emotions affect the physical body?

The body is the form that emotional frequencies flow within, like water in a river shaping its banks. If you are thinking and feeling, "Relationships hurt. Life hurts." you are sending a vibration that says, "Hurt," to the physical cellular structure of your body, until there is a medically measurable "hurt" or symptom.

The effect of waves of emotion in the various areas of the body is similar to the state of standing in front of a loud-speaker. Some broadcasts, such as high volume feedback, could make you uncomfortable and perhaps cause physical damage to your ears. Soft rhythmic tones might calm your heart rate.

For a woman who has endured great emotional stress or abuse through unhealthy relationships with men, there can be an accumulation of damaging energetic messages in her Emotional Storage and Sex Centers, which can manifest over time as physical problems with her reproductive system. For a man who has not addressed underlying issues of powerlessness and frustration from childhood, and who has instead vented that anger towards others, the toxic emotions that have been flowing through the Power and Emotional Storage Centers may form up as liver or kidney ailments.

What is stronger, love or fear?

It is more an issue of which vibration is stronger in your being. Fear may *feel* more intense, and it may be easier to fall into fear than to feel love, but that is only because your experiences have trained you to pay more attention to fear than to love.

To focus on fear is a human way of being because people learn best through pain. For survival, you need to remember what has been dangerous in the past, emotionally as well as physically. So, you pay attention to situations that trigger your fears more than to things that bring enjoyment and pleasure. Your sensitivity to fear and pain is helpful only when it warns you of real danger, not when it randomly and persistently vibrates stronger than your ability to feel good.

When you feel separation or danger, the response is an expression of fear (anger, neediness, worry, criticism, impatience, withdrawal). Fear will drive actions that lead to more anguish when you are motivated by the sensation that something terrible will happen, unless you change the situation. In contrast, you naturally receive and project the essence of love (compassion, affection, joy) if you are experiencing a sense of safety and connection.

You are, at any given moment, influenced by a blend of frequencies transmitted through your being. New vibrations are mixed with frequencies already relayed within the system, setting off reactions like a ball in a pinball machine. The essence of an old trauma bouncing back and forth through your energy centers reactivates and amplifies the old wounds and reactions until the volume of pain drowns out the broadcast of loving experiences in present time. You can turn down the Emotional Storage Center which is shouting, "old pain," and instead crank up the message of the Heart Center to the conscious mind, "receiving love now."

To be able to choose your emotions, to override your ingrained, self-protective impulses using your conscious mind and free will, is one of the greatest challenges here on Earth.

If you are struggling between love and fear, ask yourself, "Which of these feelings has more influence in my being? Which do I focus on? Which message do I listen to? Which do I feed?" Whatever you feed, love or fear, will grow.

Does our thinking affect our emotions, or do our emotions influence our thoughts?

The mind and emotions are integrally blended. When you think it, you feel it. If you feel something, you will believe it to be true. Thought is the energy that wires and designs a person's experience. Emotion is the way our perceptions and beliefs are reinforced.

Two people can experience the same thing, like being in a minor car crash, and have very unique emotional responses.

One *feels* totally victimized and angry, based on an assumption formed in their past (lots of sibling conflicts) that the driver of the other car did something *to* them. Though momentarily shaken, the other person *feels* concern for the other driver, used to thinking of others (caring for an ailing parent when growing up). Their individual engrained thought patterns cause them to have very different *feelings* in a single event. And, because of these different *feelings*, they will each have a different *belief* about what has just happened.

The mind is powerful. Viewing a situation through the filter of a previous painful experience can trick you into the false belief of danger now. Your thoughts send a warning message of *"Danger!"* with the intensity of a fire alarm, to the Heart, solar plexus, and instinctual Centers. The resounding feeling of *"fear!"* is stronger than the analysis being processed by the conscious mind that, in fact, you are safe this time. The Heart Center feels great discomfort and emotional distress. The solar plexus (Power Center) twangs with the pulse of danger, activating adrenaline. The instinctual survival Root Center creates the impulse to run. Like a freight train accelerating down a hill, the emotional response takes on its own momentum reinforcing to the mind that you are not safe.

"Am I running because I am scared? Or am I scared because I am running?"

Intentionally or not, what you think and feel, you create.

Are you saying that I have control over how I am feeling?

Part of your soul experience in a physical body is learning how to affect changes. The combination of your analytical conscious mind and your inspirational super-conscious mind brings about ideas for improving your Earth experience. You do have the ability to evaluate and transform how you feel and respond in any situation. You are a creative being.

How do I change what I think and feel?

At any given point, you are operating with a blending of subconscious, conscious and super-conscious brain functioning as well as with aspects of the emotions, ego, and physical body. Awareness of what you are receiving, interpreting, and responding to gives you control over how you perceive and respond.

For example, when in a state of confusion and emotional pain, you try to understand what is happening using your rational conscious mind, but nothing makes sense. Your present situation doesn't explain why you feel so intensely, so perhaps your system is responding to an old trauma. "Is this triggering something from the past?"

You can delve into the truth hidden away in the subconscious by asking, "What am I really afraid of? Where does that come from?" Look beyond yourself in the moment to access the soul truth of the matter. Perhaps you are dealing with someone whose disturbing behavior has nothing to do with you – to see the challenge they are facing helps you have compassion and not take in their emotions. Perhaps you can tap into the story of a past life to understand that your instincts and emotions are reacting to a perception of danger rather than a real problem – getting clues as to the source of trauma allows the fear to dissipate. Perhaps you can receive an insight about how to see it all differently. Ask your higher self, "What am I supposed to be learning here?"

To reveal the subconscious (what was) as compared to the conscious (what is), and then turn to the super-conscious (what could be), is to become open to inspiration and creativity. Change is born from the ability to wonder – a unique human quality.

Creative thought allowed the caveman to switch from eating rancid meat, "Meat taste bad." After licking a burnt finger, he began to "wonder" what would happen if the meat went in the fire. A new idea led to experimentation, evaluation, and improvement.

To shift the old patterns, you need to see the possibility of a new way beyond your present circumstance, beyond the limitations of your human frame of reference, and for that you need imagination.

Is imagination the same as inspiration? What about creative thought?

They each relate to thinking of a thing that is not yet evidenced. Often used interchangeably, the terms are more accurately defined as three parts of a process.

Imagination is the mental activity of opening to receiving a new possibility; "I wonder how this could be." To imagine is to allow an "image" in, a conscious intention to have an idea or image in your mind of something different than what already exists. To imagine is to be open to the new thing that could "pop" into your head. Imagination breaks through the limitations previously created based on your own restricted experience and frame of reference.

Inspiration is direct insight through the super-conscious, the action of Spirit energy moving inward (*in-Spir*-ation). Inspiration is a co-creative process, a blending with Universal Soul, which comes through most easily when unhampered by your conscious mind. Maybe you are busy dancing, painting, or taking a shower; something that doesn't take much mental activity – you've washed dishes a million times – and suddenly you are inspired with a solution to a sticky problem. The trick is to get your busy brain out of the way so that a free flow of vibration can be received. Inspiration is then automatically sent, like a messenger delivering a challenge to your reasoning mind that says, "What do you think about this idea? Analyze it. See if it makes sense." Inspirations received may not always be practical, but they lead to creative thought.

Creative thought is inspiration *embraced* by the conscious mind. It is the function of your mind that transforms a new idea through focus and brings that refined vision into the physical. Simple examples of using creative thought to manifest a vision include painting, music, gardening and cooking. Creative thought does not take the concentration of other conscious thought, only a willingness to play with the Power of Pretend.

What is the Power of Pretend?

The Power of Pretend recognizes attitude and perspective as the driving force of what you create in your life. What you anticipate is what you feel. What you hold in your vision manifests. With that in mind, you have the power to design a new life for yourself.

Create an image that only includes those things you want to bring into your new life, and leave behind the things that cause you pain. It is not a package deal. You get to be more selective. It is time to use your imagination. Forget limiting yourself. Forget being reasonable. Forget being realistic. It is time to use your imagination and *pretend* that you get to have a better life now, *because you do*.

***I've tried positive affirmations, but they don't
always work. How can I pretend everything is
okay when it's not?***

Positive affirmations can be effective, as they override
the noise in your head. If there is no real change, you may
only be imposing your will on a situation without addressing
the underlying issues. When you try to convince yourself of
something that you don't really believe while everything
in your being resonates with the opposite message, then you
are not working with the Power of Pretend so much as
you are in denial. You are missing important steps.

With the Power of Pretend, the first step is awareness,
the second is imagination, and the third is revised action.
You use the conscious mind (observation and attention to
truth) in partnership with the super-conscious mind (imagining
how it could be different), to avoid dwelling in the subconscious mind (the same old feelings and reinforcement of the
pattern). With a new idea to put into practice, the Power of
Pretend calls you to act and feel *as if*, while you move
forward with thoughts and actions that are in alignment with
that new idea. As you also make practical, tangible changes,
you rewire the feelings and beliefs that you hold in your
being. As those underlying thoughts and emotions are transformed, you are no longer "pretending" because things have
really become different.

As a demonstration, let's suppose that you desire a new

job to give you more work satisfaction and a better source of income. The first step is to really look at why you are in the less than desirable situation you are currently in, to evaluate your beliefs about self-worth and deserving, as well as to understand if there are unresolved issues in how you relate to others. If you are honest with yourself, you will be less inclined to recreate the same problems.

The second step is to *imagine* what a new and better job would look like for you. Not with specific details, but by focusing on the *qualities* that a different situation would bring. *Imagine* a work situation where you are getting to do what you are really good at, with people appreciating your contributions. *Imagine* showing up and feeling glad to be there, being welcomed by people who are also happy with their work. *Imagine* receiving a paycheck that is the physical demonstration of your worth and feeling valued.

Pretend that this is what you are about to step into, with confidence that such a position exists. As you hold these focused intentions and assume the feelings of having such a job, make the new connections, put out your revised resume, and do what needs to be done to let the world know you are ready to step into your new job.

If you can you imagine the opposite of now, you can create it.

What about my emotional pain? I can't just imagine that away.

Using imagination without clearing emotional pain is like putting frosting on a cake made with gravel. The deep underlying patterns of childhood and past lives may resonate stronger than your mental intentions, and continue to dictate the way you operate. The trick is to eliminate the old *and* to fill the space with something new.

Before you can "imagine it away," see if you can discover why you are still *in* emotional pain. Have you been willing to address your emotional pain at its core level, perhaps with counseling? Are there difficult circumstances that you have created in your life that warrant changing? Has your emotional pain become like a close, but bitter friend that you are resistant to abandoning? Are you comfortable with who you might be and what might fill your life *without* your emotional pain?

You can't imagine away your emotional pain, but you can use imagination, inspiration, and creative thought to change the vibrations moving through your being. You can set off a healthier chain reaction in your thoughts, feelings and responses as you tackle that emotional pain.

Isn't the goal to move beyond the physical, into the Spiritual realm?

The fact that you are in the physical is not the cause of

your problems. The imbalances in your emotions, ego, and thoughts are the source of your ongoing confusion and suffering. The goal is to embrace the spiritual while in the physical, not to judge one state as better than the other or to escape your earthly experience.

To embrace all aspects of your being gives you an opportunity to accept what is real, to imagine what is possible, and to make choices that help you thrive during your time on Earth, as a person and as a soul.

A human life is the vehicle to take your soul from where you've been to where you are going. Enjoy the ride.

SOUL AGREEMENTS

You are not alone on your Earth journey.

To feel as one, to maintain the sense of the love and support that a soul has in the Spirit realm between lives, soul family members participate in each other's lives on Earth. Having been together since their beginnings, there is a history of love and trust, a basis of shared purpose and a mutual desire to assist in each other's development.

How do soul family members help each other on this Earth journey?

Souls make agreements to play certain roles with each other, creating an avenue to approach the goals and lessons chosen for that particular lifetime.

What are these soul agreements? Why do we need them?

Soul agreements are a plan between two or more souls to interact and do something for each other. It may be to love and support; it may be to push and prod; it may be to teach or be taught.

The soul agreement holds people together as they face life lessons that might otherwise be avoided and allows for relationships of a more profound nature. Without soul agreements for relationships, events would be much more random.

When and how are agreements arranged?

Prior to coming into the physical plane, a soul might propose, "I want to learn what it is like to be crippled. Will you be an older sibling and help take care of me?" If the answer is "Yes," there may be a reciprocal agreement, such as, "And I will push you to develop unconditional love and patience." If the answer is "No, I do not want to do a life like that," the soul reevaluates. Since the experience of being crippled would be too hard without support, they choose an alternate task, or find another soul to make such an agreement.

Agreements can be simple or complex, one-way or reciprocal, harmonious or conflicting, depending upon what the individual souls are seeking to gain from an interaction. Much like life goals, agreements are made on a soul level, beyond the thought processes or emotional fears of the human personality.

When the soul agreement involves two who are of similar birth age, agreements are made in the spirit realm. Other soul agreements are made when one is already in the physical, such as parent and child, grandparent and child, or teacher and student.

A soul family group may reincarnate together over the course of several generations, switching roles while maintaining a commitment of support. Following is an example of two souls doing a leap-frog of lifetimes: Clara lived from 1905 until 1990. Her soul challenges stemmed from a difficult childhood with a mother who was unable to protect her from abuse. She was the grandmother of Elizabeth who was born in 1963. They shared an easy relationship, and in her old age, Clara was grateful for Elizabeth's compassion and devotion as she cared for her. After her life as Clara, her soul communicated on the astral plane, with Elizabeth's soul, asking to be born as her daughter. "I need to embrace another challenge with the soul of that abusive father, in order to break the cycle and take back my power. With you as my mother, I will have the unconditional love and support I need."

The relationship would also bring the personal growth Elizabeth needed, so her soul agreed to the arrangement and her daughter Maria was born. As Maria (Clara) once again

---

suffered abuse in childhood, Elizabeth and her extended family were instrumental both emotionally and financially in helping her break through her old victim pattern. In the process of helping her daughter, Elizabeth developed the wisdom and strength she needed for herself. Both had chosen the right partner to accomplish their tasks and achieve balance on a soul level.

Are energy cords and soul agreements related?

Agreements are a soul intention to connect. Energy cords "seal the deal." Soul agreements are made on the astral, as a reciprocal plan to accomplish some sort of task together, while energy cords are an aspect of the physical plane, the extra and intangible link that enables you to do so. A cord can serve as an additional flow of love between two hearts or as the tie that binds you together until you have learned a difficult lesson. As an extension of the soul agreement, energy cords connect automatically when you meet in the physical. When the task is complete, or if the interaction is unworkable, you move on from that soul agreement, and so the energy cords between you are no longer necessary or advisable.

Who do we make soul agreements with?

In a reciprocal agreement between two souls, you will chose a soul who is suited to a particular role and is also willing. "You can do what I need and I can do what you need."

Through previous interaction with each other, you gain a sense of character. Does their nature fit with the type of interaction you require?

Some souls are mature enough for unconditional love and will not abandon the task at hand. Others are still focusing on their own needs, and will likely play the role of child or student. You may make an agreement with the same soul to be your mother several times because you are trusting of her devotion. If you take turns, experiencing opposite roles with the same soul, you'll see what it is like to be in the other's position.

Agreements are made with soul family members as well as those outside of the comfort and familiarity of that group.

What is the difference between soul family and non-soul family in regard to making agreements?

The bonds and commitments are stronger in a soul family agreement, while agreements with non-soul family members provide an opportunity to stretch your experiences beyond the security of the familiar.

Soul family will have a natural interest in their members' growth and development. Since the progress of the group as a whole depends upon each individual's learning, soul family members tend to be more devoted and less likely to abandon an agreement once it is begun.

Like young children, souls in their earliest lives need the

safety of soul family members as they learn about the world. As souls mature, they branch into a few interactions with souls they have not encountered before while still having the home base of the soul family. Eventually, as experience, knowledge and skills increase, there is an expansion to connecting with those outside of the family.

Choosing to have agreements within the soul family, or not, depends upon the type of tasks a soul is taking on.

What kind of agreements do we make?

Some soul agreements are designed to balance out events or emotions from another life, while others bring about totally new experiences and challenges.

For healing and nurturing from previous trauma, you need gentle and loving agreements to sustain your willingness to participate, like having someone to hold your hand through a scary movie. If you need to be toughened up or humbled, there will be an adversary to relentlessly challenge you, becoming like "the sand in the oyster that makes the pearl grow." To undo a pattern of violence, you may work on simply leaving each other alone.

To learn the opposite, you will take turns. "I was your teacher before, so now I will be your student and you will teach me." By understanding what it feels like in both positions, you gain compassion for others. "First I was abusive. Now, having been the victim, I know how terrible it feels to be powerless, so I won't do that anymore."

To attempt something you haven't tried before, you may step into a unique situation. "I have been weak in many lives. Now, I would like to see what it is like to master physical strength." The soul chooses a family of athletes, in which not only the genetics, but also the group focus is on developing their bodies. An agreement is formed with the father, intolerant of "quitters" who will push the son to achieve his maximum potential.

To challenge an old dynamic, you may slightly alter the soul agreements and scenario, giving a better possibility of accomplishment. A woman has a relationship with a man whereby she spends her life overpowered and dominated. Her soul, desiring to overcome the pattern of low self-worth from that life, chooses another love relationship with the same soul. This time, she will have first been raised in an environment that teaches her independence and empowerment. So, she makes additional agreements with a self-sufficient mother and an encouraging mentor. With this support, she can approach such a challenging union from a position of strength and personal equilibrium.

You also set up agreements with those who will support your soul path. A soul who is embracing the role of a leader forms an agreement with parents who will provide an environment of education and siblings who will give experience with the struggles between conflicting personalities. The life partner will be encouraging and share the burden of public service. A soul wishing to bring a great vision to the world makes an agreement with someone to provide financial assistance, without obligation. For a soul to accomplish selflessly helping others, there will be agreements with those who are suffering or struggling, giving an opportunity to learn how to be of assistance.

The goals that a soul sets for itself in any given life are complex. Multiple and interwoven soul agreements ensure that there is always someone to play off of.

Are soul agreements always between individual souls, or are there group agreements?

Soul family members may have shared goals and group agreements. When souls have endured trauma or hardship as a group, as in cultural poverty or genocide, those souls may return in subsequent lives with the task of healing or empowering the whole. Multiple souls may also form group agreements to improve a situation, such as a community uniting to overthrow a tyrant, changing prosperity for future generations and achieving an ongoing shift for many in the soul family.

Groups of souls may also help each other in ways that may appear horrific. Warriors fighting each other may be an agreement between soul family members to learn about power through violence without drawing others into the situation.

What about souls who take on a role with not just one or two others, but who seem to be acting out the same role for a large group of people, like government leaders?

There are souls with a grand scale life task who first make agreements to receive support or challenge in order to develop the qualities and circumstances they will need to make a major difference in the world. They also make agreements with the group of souls who will be impacted by their actions.

There are the obvious benefactors of the masses, inventing medicines or improving economic conditions. But even when a soul's actions seem to be detrimental to the group, they may be serving their agreement through the trouble they cause. By "waking" people up, they compel sweeping changes that bring balance. Famous people with tragic lifestyles and drug addictions may have an agreement to bring awareness to widespread social problems that would otherwise go unnoticed. Politicians draw attention to scandalous corruption in government by being caught in the act.

Not every action is tied to an agreement, but there is often more going on than the apparent human struggle.

What about suffering? Am I being punished for something I did before?

You are not required to endure suffering. You have the right to choose which situations are valuable and which are only causing pain. Sometimes, you are still needing to learn something as inspired by your current challenge, while other times it is in your best interest to let go and move on.

Punishment is a human concept developed out of the fact that people tend to learn best through some degree of suffering. Pain makes more of an impact than comfort. There may be something that your soul's design is trying to teach you, but you are not enduring struggle now because you are "bad."

The term karma describes the concept that if you do a thing in one life, that you will have that same thing done to you in another. The goal is to learn to live well, so it does not serve your soul to be trapped in tit-for-tat balancing. There is another way.

For instance, a soul exploring what it is like to be ruthless and greedy has an experience as an 1850's California gold miner. His lust for instant gratification and disregard for others knows no limits. In a rash but characteristic move, he steals his partner's gold and sets fire to the building where he is sleeping. He creates an "unfortunate accident," with no accountability or remorse in that life. For balance, he could choose a life of suffering at the hands of those once wronged, but this soul chooses instead to take on a life of service. Born now, into a financially stable and loving family, he has become a gregarious and generous man. Working as a paramedic provides the setting to set aside his own safety while rescuing others from harm. He has retained a sense of adventure, but instead of taking advantage, he is assisting others. Perhaps he will help the same souls he had harmed in the past, perhaps not, but a certain volume of service accumulates to balance acts of greed and violence, accomplished without suffering, blame or punishment.

What happens if I bail on a soul agreement?

Soul agreements are not binding. They can always be renegotiated.

Situations on Earth do not always turn out the way souls anticipate – a family move separates you from a supportive friend, a parent becoming crippled eliminates the opportunity for advanced education, a childhood influence leads you into trouble. If one or both of you fail to develop a quality you needed for the task, the agreement will be too difficult to accomplish.

In any situation, a person can only do what they are capable of. Have you done your best? What will you do differently next time?

How do I know when to leave a soul agreement relationship that's too hard?

If the relationship is causing a disproportionate amount of trouble and pain compared to the love, companionship, or growth, it may be time to move on, even if the agreement is not complete. Sometimes one soul has accomplished their part while the other resists. Sometimes neither is able to embrace the agreement and it is better to not hold each other back.

If I can't manage to get along with someone in this life, do we have to keep coming into lives together until we can?

Soul agreements are negotiated on a life by life basis. There is always the option to try again, but there is no mandatory obligation.

For example, a soul who made an agreement to be of support to you grows up in a dysfunctional family. This disrupts their emotional growth to the point where they are lost in the reckless behavior of an addiction instead of being able to help you. After a subsequent life receiving healthier imprinting, that same soul may have the maturity and self-sufficiency required to accomplish the original task. In which case, your souls agree to try again in a new life setting.

Understand that you will not endure some future life penance for avoiding a relationship of conflict now. You are not required to get along with everyone, but even the most difficult interactions become easier when you understand what is going on.

Is every encounter we have based on a soul agreement?

Relationships of any substance have underlying soul

agreements, but a person also has random encounters as part of the experience of being here. There does not have to be a prearranged plan for a person to benefit from an encounter, but agreements are helpful to ensure that certain lessons will be presented.

Are intense relationships an indication of a soul agreement?

Soul agreements are not always intense, and relationships with an intense connection do not always indicate a soul agreement.

You may be caught in a loop of behavior from the past – a role carryover. Being stuck in the roles that were played for an agreement in a previous life can interfere with what you are attempting to accomplish in a new soul agreement or keep you enmeshed even when there is no agreement in the current life.

For example, when you meet a soul who betrayed you in another life, there is a tendency to revert to how you used to relate. Not having received any new instructions for behavior (if there is no direct agreement in this life), their soul seems to be saying, "Here you are again. You are the one I agreed to betray. I will do that." Even if there *is* a new agreement to be of assistance in *this* life, they may prefer the position of power again. And it is easy for *your* soul, having been accustomed to betrayal, to be taken advantage of again.

Reenacting the old pattern is harmful to both. If changing the way you respond does not shift the relationship, it is better to avoid the interaction.

How do I know if I have completed a soul agreement or not?

In the beginning of a soul agreement connection, there is a passionate drive to connect. At the end, there is no juice. Friends who simply part ways because there is nothing of common interest any longer, the end of a benefactor's financial support, a nemesis whose previous aggravating actions no longer elicit the same emotional reaction, or the absence of the once strong impulse to take care of someone.

The people can go their separate ways, or they may choose to shift into a less profound relationship. In other cases, one may have the understanding to move on, but the other has a hard time adapting to the change or letting go.

Do we often make agreements with a soul for more than one life?

Though agreements are made one life at a time, two souls may end up helping each other through a series of lives as they make the progression from focusing on survival needs to working together for the good of the group.

Two souls begin an agreement in a life where food is scarce and they must compete to survive. Being hungry and seeing that the other has food, one hits the other over the head with a stick. "Bonk! You're dead! I steal your meat!" The next life, the situation plays out in reverse. Each of them has had the experience of killing and being killed over food, to see what that is like. In subsequent lives, they take turns being the parent providing food for the other, learning the benefits of love and sharing. "You give *me* food, and it makes *me* happy. I give *you* food and it makes *you* happy. I now trust you to care about me."

Later, their soul agreements create opportunities to expand on the concept of cooperation." They live in a community not related by blood where their two families are at odds with each other. At first they act out in competitive ways, feuding over land rights, only remembering the benefit of sharing (on a soul level) when they are forced to band together to fight a fire sweeping over both their lands. Eventually, their agreement is fully harmonious, as they team up to create a company with a focus on civic philanthropy. In ever increasing complexity, the theme of learning to take care of each other is explored and developed.

As our soul evolves, how do our agreements change?

Your beginning lives are filled with agreements which create learning through pain and struggle as you gather basic knowledge of how the world operates; what is dangerous and what is safe. Middle lives involve a mix of soul agree-

---

ments, making new mistakes to learn from while working to correct previous imbalances. Toward the end of a soul's cycle of lives, soul agreements present opportunities for clearing any unresolved issues and for teaching or assisting others. As the soul progresses, dealing less with painful lessons or emotional carryovers, agreements with other souls shift from struggle to support and help actualize the accomplishment of the soul purpose.

Perhaps a soul is experimenting with the various aspects of being a warrior. At first, the person will kill others, just so that the soul can experience the power and ruthlessness of unfeeling violence. In the next lives, there will be agreements so that he learns what it feels like to be randomly killed. In another life, the soul has agreements to go battle others, but only with an important cause. In subsequent agreements, he will be struck down by those who are equally driven in their purpose.

As the warrior soul evolves, agreements still involve conflicts, but of a less physical nature. Emotions are now the battleground – romantic betrayal, sibling rivalry, and parental domination. Eventually, after experiencing both sides of each, lives of emotional retaliation give way to agreements that offer healing. "I hurt you, so you hurt me," changes to "I hurt you, so now I will help you." The lover, once unfaithful, returns through an agreement to be devoted, loving and supportive of the other's life goals.

Because of inexperience and rash behavior, your soul initially accumulates emotional carryovers – traumatic memories can trigger fears and responses in a later life. Agreements in subsequent lives often serve to release and heal those associations. To help you overcome the pattern caused by abuse, you may make agreements through a series of lives. The first interaction may be a soft and gentle love, nurturing, but limiting your growth with dependency. The next agreement teaches you to develop self-worth and autonomy, while a later relationship challenges your old fears and tests your ability to stand up for yourself. Eventually, when you are strong and clear, you have relationship agreements for love of an enduring and balanced nature.

Not only do the *types* of agreements you make change, but *whom* you make agreements with changes. You start out making agreements with those of the same soul age and development. In time, as your soul progresses, you are able to relate to and learn from agreements with souls of all levels.

Does our connection to the soul family change as we progress?

At the beginning of lives, souls incarnate into birth families with only their soul family members. "I am the way I am, and I need to be with people just like me." To move beyond the insulation of safety, you need to learn to get along with others you do not innately understand.

The first step towards progression is to make agreements for a birth family that is comprised of all soul family members except one, a soul you have not encountered before. Gradually, your birth family agreements are a mix of soul family and not. As an older soul, you form agreements only with souls outside of the soul family. The soul lesson of being born into a family that does not welcome you as a soul family member is to be able to love yourself and the others unconditionally even though they may be averse to you. "I am the way I am, and they are the way they are. I need to recognize the difference and accept it."

For those older souls who start out with extremely difficult birth families, there will be agreements to meet up later in life with others who are of their soul family – "*Now* I feel at home" – to balance the previous disassociation with joyful reunion and acceptance.

As the general population of the planet embraces the challenge of making agreements beyond the comfort of their soul family, some will live harmoniously with others very different from themselves, while others will fail miserably and cause a great deal of turmoil in the human social structure.

Beyond the birth family, do we make agreements with souls who are not of the soul family?

Yes. When no one from the soul family is willing or available to participate for a specific task, an arrangement will be made with someone else. If you only need a brief encounter, as in learning to face a job interview that goes badly, someone outside of the soul family is best, because you will be less emotionally impacted. When you desire to experience life in a particular geographic location, which is different than that of your soul family, your remaining options for agreements will be with non-soul family members. Choosing a soul family member, or not, is part of determining what you need to do, and how it will work with one soul or another.

How can you tell if an agreement is with a soul family member or not? Are harmonious and loving relationships an indication of a soul family connection?

Yes, loving, nurturing and supportive relationships are usually agreements with soul family members, but difficult interactions can be as well.

People often assume that if their relationship is challenging, instead of harmonious, that it must not be a soul family connection. But when you have a lesson which requires someone to push you (unfinished business, toughening up, overcoming old patterns, or being tested), there needs to be an underlying bond of love and familiarity like you have with a soul family member. Otherwise, you would simply run away and not experience what your soul requires.

Does a soul ever choose to have a life of no agreements at all with their soul family?

Most souls prefer their growth be with the soul family, but some do choose a life away from that love and support. Much like Dorothy, in *The Wizard of Oz*, a time of separation teaches appreciation. "There's no place like home."

Also, when a soul has evolved to a point that it can interact well with all, soul family or not, agreements can easily be with either.

Does a soul ever become permanently estranged from the soul family?

Very rarely, but there are cases where a soul has a series of dropped agreements, becomes trapped in lust and power, or causes more harm than good in their interactions, causing their soul family to avoid participation in agreements. Though not permanently, they'll be left to work with non-soul family members before they are ready for such a challenge of unfamiliarity.

Soul family estrangement can teach valuable lessons, but it may also perpetuate a spiral loop of isolation, with lives filled with more anger, alienation and pain. But regardless of what happens during human lives, the soul family will always be there on the astral to assist with the healing a soul needs between lives.

Are new souls ever brought into existing soul families?

No. Shared experience from the beginning is the basis of soul family love and support, so it would not serve a soul to be introduced later. They would always be an outsider.

Do all souls within a soul family group evolve at the same rate?

Even though souls begin their sequence of lives together, there is variety in the quality and number of lives lived, so soul family members will evolve at different rates.

Souls with more experience are likely to have achieved more soul growth, but the number of lives does not correlate exactly with the amount of evolution. A soul can come to Earth twenty times, choosing relatively easy lessons, and not have much challenge or growth. Meanwhile, another soul could live only five times with intense experiences that push them to develop far beyond the others.

A variety of soul ages within the soul family expands the scenarios and agreements possible. Those who have mastered a particular task assist those who are still learning, accelerating the evolution of the entire group. A soul who has achieved balance in the use of power facilitates the challenge a younger one is grappling with – like a sword-master showing an apprentice warrior how to be skillful and strong without resorting to abuse or dominance.

By the time a number of souls have evolved to the point of completing their cycle of lives, others are midway along, while a few linger at much earlier levels of growth. This great diversity of progress essentially divides the soul family into subgroups.

What are soul family subgroups?

Souls who develop at the same pace and work together towards a specific goal over a series of lives form into subgroups. After a time, even though they are all from the original soul family, souls will have more affinity with those in their subgroup than with those they have had little interaction with.

Comparing the soul family to a very large extended family, the subgroups are the nuclear family units. After a sequence of lives, the subgroups may reorganize into different combinations, like all the children going in one direction while the parents go in another.

To illustrate, a soul family of two hundred and forty comes to Earth. Eighty souls begin a sequence of lives in a tribe in Africa, keeping to themselves through eight or nine generations. Another seventy live several generations as nomadic desert wanderers, then integrate with those from a subgroup of ninety souls who have been living in sub arctic climates. The seventy and ninety, now make an interactive group of one hundred and sixty, evolving at a more accelerated rate than the segregated subgroup of eighty, because they are exposed to a greater variety of personalities, environments, and soul agreements. Eventually, forty souls from each of the three groups incarnate together during a series of two or three generations in an urban city in Japan, while thirty from each of the three groups have experiences together through a sequence of lives in rural Russia.

Subgroups with a common endeavor may operate as a tight-knit unit throughout their entire cycle of lives or only for a few incarnations. Members of the same subgroup can also learn individually, undergoing similar challenges in different environments – one soul living as a slave woman in India, one as a Chinese servant and another as a Blacksmith's apprentice, each embracing the lesson of subservience on their own before reuniting with their shared knowledge in a new life where they work together as a team.

Is that why someone from the soul family might feel like a stranger?

When souls follow their unique paths and focus on dissimilar lessons, there will be less familiarity and recognition – much like two siblings who don't relate as adults. "I feel a connection with you and I care about you, but I don't understand you anymore."

When you are kindred souls in many lifetimes, your rapport will have the harmony of a beautiful song. If you are distanced by a difference in soul age or experience, you will have little in common.

Souls from different subgroups may not feel like the same soul family, but the connection between lives sustains the closeness.

Do soul agreements last for a whole life, or do we have different kinds as we move from childhood to adulthood?

There are phases you move through, with simultaneous agreements for challenge and acceptance. Some agreements only serve you for a particular lesson, while the ones of loving support are beneficial through out an entire life.

Initially, during your childhood training, you have agreements to toughen you up, teach you skills, hone your talents, and develop latent qualities that would not occur otherwise. Being given responsibility, as a teenager, to care for an elderly relative (soul agreements with grandparent and parents) will develop the skills of patience and compassion needed for a later agreement to care for your handicapped child. There are also agreements that seem cruel, but teach you what you'll need for your life purpose. To be neglected will bring self-sufficiency, an important characteristic for a pioneering leader. Being teased by a sibling will provide the experience of toughening one's skin, a quality needed to present innovative and controversial social ideas to the world.

Childhood soul agreements present an opportunity to balance emotional carryovers from past lives – similar situations and associations trigger the memories. A person you have had many lives of deadly conflict with shows up as a competitive brother, a chance for you both to evolve your way of relating beyond the stage of killing each other. Another scenario is the mother who is overly protective in this life in contrast to when her soul abandoned you in another life.

Once the childhood training and balancing are complete, agreements of conflict and challenge are no longer useful. Children move into independent adult lives, and siblings go their different ways. Relationship patterns can continue beyond their value, and it is then a matter of acknowledging that you are done. "I am tough enough. I no longer need anyone to pick on me." Some soul agreements endure as reminders of the lessons previously learned. If your father was constantly critical and yet, you have learned not to take it personally, when he says something negative towards you, you make note of how his attitude no longer affects you and get to see how far you've come.

After the childhood training, agreements for adult interactions begin, reinforcing what has been accomplished or presenting what still needs balancing. A marriage with a person who is possessive and controlling may be your test to see how you have overcome the disempowerment learned from an overly protective mother. To have a boss who is decadent and dishonest may be an agreement to remind you what can happen in a life of greed such as when you were the murdered wife of a corrupt politician.

From a human perspective, these trials may feel like you are just being subjected to more victimization or punishment, but there is a purpose. Agreements that test and remind are designed to keep you from repeating past ways of weakness, give you an opportunity to make healthier choices, and signal the soul that you have learned what you need in order to embrace your more worldly tasks.

You have a choice to hold anger and resentment toward souls who have caused you pain, or to take inventory of the important skills and qualities you would not have without those tough agreements. Then you move into soul agreements that are easier and assist you with your life purpose: the mentor who comes along to advance your science career, the love partner who cherishes you and sets you free, the business partner who helps you to develop your prosperous invention, or the series of employers who launch you into a powerful position of leadership.

Is there a special kind of soul agreement with twins? Is that different than agreements with other kinds of siblings?

As examples of how the world operates, siblings give us

an opportunity to test out behaviors and see what happens. Agreements with brothers and sisters are directly designed to prepare us for what is to come later.

With siblings, there can be an agreement to come together for companionship and support, a challenging rivalry, or a combination of both. Locked in the same family, there is little chance that a sibling will avoid the agreement, at least during childhood.

Sharing the womb sets up an even tighter situation. The twins agreement is set up either for extreme support, "I can't do this alone. You have to be right here with me," or to force you to transcend your differences. "We were enemies before. If we are the same, maybe we can understand each other." Having matching physical characteristics creates a mirror to see yourself as not separate from another.

Are soul agreements always mutual, or can one impose it on the other?

One soul cannot force another soul into an agreement without at least some degree of consent. The level of coercion or reluctance will influence whether or not the agreement is actualized. The weaker the consent, the more likely a soul is to give up when things get difficult.

A classic scenario of a non-agreement is one where an impatient soul launches into life with a mother who is reluctant to take the child on. Rather than seeing her light at conception as an invitation to explore agreement possibilities, the incoming soul assumes a commitment.

In some cases of imposition, parent souls will adjust and make agreements while the baby is in the womb, the child lives a life without the connections it seeks, or there is no birth.

Does that mean that if a pregnancy ends through miscarriage or abortion, that there was no soul agreement?

No. Generally speaking, miscarriage results when a body is conceived but no soul agrees to come in, when the baby's soul opts out, or there is a physical problem.

Abortion without a soul agreement can be the mother's soul saying, "I am not the one for you," or "Now is not the right time." There are also cases when abortion is breaking a soul agreement, and the soul will have to find another (mother) soul to make an agreement with. Once a mother/child soul connection is made, the soul who intended to come in may wait until there is another pregnancy with that same mother.

When a pregnancy ends, either by miscarriage or abortion, there are consequences for all involved and the decision is not to be taken lightly. But the ultimate commitment to bring a soul into the world – for baby or mother – is made on a soul level.

What about the case of rape, child abandonment, or adoption? What kinds of soul agreements are involved in those scenarios?

All situations are unique and complex. There may be a soul agreement that has been renegotiated or broken, a soul agreement that is being carried out, or no soul agreement at all.

Rape may be a case of a soul seeking a life of early emotional hardship making an agreement with a mother who will be angry and embittered instead of welcoming. When pregnancy through rape is not part of the woman's soul intentions, one of her soul family may choose to come in as her child, forming an agreement to help her transform victimization into unconditional love.

Adoption is often the case of a soul (baby) making agreements with one set of parents for the desired physical, genetic characteristics and another for family setting, upbringing, and childhood opportunities. When a mother changes her mind at birth, not giving up the child as intended during pregnancy, those secondary soul agreements are upset. It is also possible that the mother choosing to keep her baby could be keeping an agreement, instead of disrupting the soul path, as the intended adoption would do. Whatever the soul agreement, to adopt out or not, if the plan changes at birth, those involved will need to adjust greatly to such an important change.

Abandonment of a child by a parent may be part of a prearranged soul plan, including agreements with others who take on the care-taking roles of step-parent, grandparent, or foster parent. Or the parent may be creating great hardship by breaking the agreement. The emotional and practical ramifications of being deserted may bring unanticipated challenges beyond the soul's capacity to cope or achieve life goals.

Children who lose their parents and either die from neglect or remain as orphans may be following a soul plan for such a life, or not. A child living in an orphanage may be exploring what life is like as one of the deprived masses (perhaps in contrast to a previous experience being spoiled and elite).

In a series of lives, two souls may take turns abandoning and being abandoned, or abandoning and then being devoted, in order to learn and balance. Adapting to the loss of parents and expanding beyond the comfort of a loving family is often the experiential lesson of an older soul.

Even with a design for a particular birth choice, there are times on Earth when unforeseen events such as war, natural disasters, accidents, and disease, cause children to be orphaned. When a child/soul loses the emotional and physical support of parents, and also important agreements, the soul is forced to choose: wallow in despair and helplessness, or shift to embracing the unscheduled opportunity.

Choices people make to bring a child into the world and parent, or not, for whatever reason, have a chain reaction along the soul paths of those involved. When you understand the soul agreements behind any particular parent child relationship, you are more likely to make choices in alignment with the soul and less likely to make harsh judgment.

Why do we need to know about agreements? If they are made on a soul level, what does it matter in our lives?

Insight into your soul agreements helps you to see why people act they way they do and to have awareness when you respond in ways totally contrary to your intellectual reason. Understanding what is happening, from a soul perspective, leads to a greater ability to improve the way you live.

For example: A woman held onto much bitterness after a disappointing love affair. At first, the two were incredibly passionate and drawn together with common interests, feeling as though they had found "the one." But during the next two years, she ended up carrying the financial burden as he pursued college, and was being excluded from his life socially, emotionally, and intimately. Knowing she should end it, she still felt obligated to try. Then, without explanation, the time came when she felt no more attraction, no willingness to do any more. She made him leave.

For many years, she was fixed in resentment, feeling

rejected and beating herself up for having wasted her time, love, and money, until she uncovered the soul truth that set her free. In a previous life, she had been an impoverished young mother in India, with no way to feed herself or her toddler son. Sick and delirious from lack of nourishment, the mother abandoned her child who soon died. In this life, she and the soul of the infant son had a new agreement to meet and balance the past. Instead of neglect, her focus would be to launch him into a prosperous and successful life.

She came to realize why it had been so natural for her to assume the role of provider, without reciprocation. When he had accomplished enough schooling to continue on his own, she had stopped taking care of him. Just like a mother and son.

She began to feel better about their interaction, seeing that she had set right a past trauma, as well as helping a soul family member attain a life goal. Seeing the bigger picture healed the bitterness and confusion that her previous limited view of human drama had created.

So far, all of my relationships seem like tough lessons and pain. Is there really a soul family out there that will feel **good***?*

In the earliest part of your life, there were many relationships to challenge and strengthen you, to teach you what you needed to know – the childhood training and testing.

Whether it was pleasant, or not, you can look back and see what you needed then to become who you are now. There are soul family who are part of this training and testing, and others whose agreements are to love and support, to help you shift out of your past and move forward toward your greater joy and work in the world.

You are in charge of the kinds of relationships that you draw to you. You have been all along. When you needed challenging interactions to make you stretch, you got them. When you needed soul family members to march you a few steps farther along your path, they were there.

To switch to soul family agreements of ease and affection, ask yourself,

"Have I had enough of encounters that push me and make me grow?"

The soul's journey is a group adventure to be shared and enjoyed with a rich variety of encounters. If it were more valuable to go through life alone, you would each have shown up on your own little island!

LOVE PARTNERS

To Be As Angels For Each Other

There is a human desire for profound union. Through the bonds of romantic love and sexuality, you peel away the illusion that you are a solitary soul and remember your divine essence. For however long a connection lasts, whether a brief moment or a lifetime, merging with another person turns life into a glorious experience. You are then able to transcend the mundane through the communion of love.

Most relationships don't fit this ideal love. What's going on?

Beyond the human drive for love, and the attraction that brings you together, there is also an underlying bond that is formed as part of a soul agreement. As you take on soul tasks you might otherwise run away from (like relationships which force you to grow), the magnetic attraction of love is the glue that holds you together. The desire for emotional connection and physical touch adds extra potency and motivation to the dynamic.

Each person has arranged for multiple possibilities with a number of souls, each to fulfill a specific interaction with the other, in order to accomplish a certain goal. Even if the human personalities aren't aware of the underlying agreement, or if the relationship becomes twisted, enmeshed, or devoid of affection, the deeper soul bond exists.

Agreements can be pleasant and long-lasting or tumultuous and short-lived, but all relationships present gifts and challenges, depending upon what your soul and personality need next. Some are designed as the gentle support you want to feel along your journey, while others force you to stretch. There are partners who will lead you to new opportunities or experiences, while others will provide security and stability. Some connections bring gentle companionship, while others present ongoing struggle.

Why are so many relationships painful failures?

Like climbing a staircase to reach a higher level, each difficult relationship is a step taken to get you from who you once were, at the beginning, to who you became by the end. You have grown with each step.

You cannot go back and change a disappointing relationship, but you can choose how you view it. Instead of focusing on pain, blame, or shame, look back over your "failed" relationships and see how each one brought a specific lesson, a shift to your awareness and abilities. Even if a painful experience simply taught you what to avoid, there is an opportunity to see what you have accomplished. From the soul perspective, the relationship is not a failure.

What do you accomplish on a soul level that would make a troubled relationship seem okay?

There are a sequence of different types of soul agreements that anyone goes through as they transition from relationships that bring agony to the more exalted unions – all opportunities to share, love, and grow.

What kinds of relationships?

Most people begin with a series of *soul growth relationship agreements*, romantic encounters which compel a certain strength, talent or quality to be acquired by either encouraging or challenging (which ever is more effective). Like childhood agreements, you are developing what you will need in order to achieve your life goals.

Some lessons can be learned gently, as when one person is an example of how to be, while other lessons are best learned by having to address that which you resist the most. If you are rigid about self-gratification, your desire to stay in a relationship may shift your priorities and enable you to put another's needs before your own. If you are too passive

---

and need to learn not to be bullied, your love relationship may push you to assert your authority.

Emotionally charged connections force you to master whatever skill you might be lacking: learning how to ask for what you need, creating your own financial self-sufficiency, or becoming aware of who to avoid. Just like falling and skinning your knees a few times as you are learning to ride a bike, with each experience you become wiser, stronger, and more skilled, even if it hurts.

There are also *soul balancing relationship agreements* where two people come together to complete some kind of unfinished business. The agreement may be to assist with balancing an extreme from childhood, such as providing financial stability to one whose early life was impoverished. A love relationship with a kind and reliable person helps overcome insecurity and mistrust caused by a sibling who liked to trick you. Your lover could be fulfilling an agreement to correct a previous failure from an earlier lifetime. "I was your husband and treated you badly. This time I'll be devoted and responsible."

Balancing agreements vary in their degree of struggle versus loving support depending upon the tasks to be accomplished and the personalities involved. Relationships can be everything from a harmonious compatibility that nurtures latent talents to a hostile environment compelling you to get tougher than you ever imagined.

Why do I keep attracting the same kinds of relationships?

Perhaps you are not quite finished with a particular challenge of growth – learning is done in incremental steps. Or you could be encountering *soul growth testing agreements*, to test the skills you have developed, in the interest of becoming confident and trusting yourself to make the right choices.

Instead of beating yourself up for what you are attracting, focus on how you are now behaving differently. As you respond to old patterns in healthier ways, you have proof that you can embrace a gloriously powerful love relationship without repeating the earlier mistakes.

In a series of relationships with controlling partners, a woman was learning how to overcome giving her power away, each time getting a little stronger and smarter. Then she had a few romantic relationships where the soul agreement was to test her resolve, to prove to her what she had accomplished. As she learned to step away graciously, before major enmeshment or conflict, she was able to trust that she would no longer get lost in destructive relationships.

The next step in ending unhealthy relationship patterns is, when encountering the same kind of person or relationship dynamic, instead of being attracted, you are not even interested. That is when you are done.

Looking back on my past love relationships, I can see what I did for them. But what did I get besides pain?

Love relationships are two-way agreements, where each has a specific role or task to perform for the other. One person is a helper while the other is a challenger. One may be teaching while the other is undoing an injustice from the past. One may be soothing a childhood wound while the other is relentlessly testing previously learned lessons.

The relationship may seem unfair in the midst of human dramas and emotional frustrations, but there is balance on a soul level. "If you do this for me, I will do that for you."

A woman is in a relationship with a man for several years, during which time she handles the accounting and advertising of his business, greatly improving his financial success. Even though he does nothing inappropriate, intimacy with him triggers her repressed memories of childhood incest. Even though she becomes withdrawn and blaming, she keeps working for him and he keeps being solid and loving. Her role in the soul agreement was to be devoted to helping him make progress in his business. His role was to continue being kind and supportive, as an example of a "good" man, to help her heal her past.

A man marries a woman who then becomes disabled and totally dependent upon him. As he takes care of her, they balance a time when she was an older sister tending to a crippled sibling (him). He learns how to be unconditionally loving and devoted, and she learns how to deal with feeling powerless.

A woman, who has struggled with betrayal in relationships, becomes involved with a man who sneaks money from her accounts. Without losing her loving composure, she makes him leave, instead of repeating her earlier mistake of allowing bad behavior to continue – she passed the boundaries test. He learns what happens when you choose money over love, without being able to transfer blame to a woman reacting in anger.

Agreements always involve service to the other. Sometimes the assistance is obvious, as when one provides financial or emotional support. Other times, what you perceive as mistreatment – conflict, confusion, betrayal, disappointment – is actually service, forcing you to change what you would not have otherwise. Understanding what is happening on the soul level helps you see the value of any relationship, even if you endure a little unhappiness in the process.

Why can't we accomplish the growth and balancing with other people and save romantic relationships just for love?

You come together because you need love. What better way to ensure that you do what is necessary to evolve as souls, to learn and grow as healthier human beings, than to be with someone who loves you, who you know and trust, on a soul level. Even if the human personality doesn't recognize the quality of this love and devotion, the soul does. There is much more going on than a simple desire for love, though that is what drives you to connect.

The ability to create children adds another level of complexity to love relationships and the soul agreements behind them. In some cases, a couple's connection may fill a lifetime, continuing even after the children are raised. Other times, the soul agreement only lasts until the parenting is complete – after providing a certain environment and the children are grown, they separate and begin new lives. The partner soul agreement may be short term, while the agreements with children continue, parenting separately – a soul wants to have several environments to grow up in, first with both, then with one parent, then with the other. Other parenting agreements are specifically to create a body for the child, and there is no soul purpose to be together as a couple except for that brief encounter.

How do you know when a relationship agreement is complete?

When a soul growth, balancing, or testing agreement begins, there is an intense draw, a feeling like you are "supposed" to be together. Attraction may be blended with anxiety, dread, excitement, a wild sense of danger, or the kind of giddy euphoria that masks the sensing of emotional conflict ahead.

But, when a soul agreement between lovers is complete, there will no longer be the magnetic pull to be together. One person may hang on, out of need or habit, but you have "fallen out" of love. Once you have accomplished a certain level of growth, you may turn around and see the other in an entirely new way, wondering why you ever connected with them (or fought with them) in the first place.

The whole love thing is so painful and confusing! What am I doing wrong?

If you do not have a strong idea about what your needs are, or what kind of person it will take to meet those needs, you may "fall in love" with whomever comes along. If you have a low opinion about what you are capable of attracting or deserve to have in a relationship, you may take whatever you can get. If you look to another to solve your problems or fill a need that you should be taking care of for yourself, you are picking someone for the wrong reasons. Either way, you will be disappointed, and cause a disservice to the other because you will wish that they were other than they are capable of being.

The goal is to work through confusion towards under-standing, of yourself and each other. Refocus your energies on taking care of what needs changing in your life – dealing with the unhealthy patterns, fears, and false beliefs from childhood and past experiences – and then your soul will no longer attract the type of relationships that force you to grow.

Refocus on the soul essence, rather than human frailties. Let go of obsessive enmeshment with a person as the path to feeling love. Become tough enough to hold a feeling of peace and calm inside, to source your own sense of being loved.

To whatever degree you have attained wholeness, you will attract one who is a reflection of your level of development. To that end, people get into a variety of love partnerships which give them the opportunity to gain strength and clarity, often times going through a series of short-lived relationship struggles to get there.

If I haven't had a relationship in a long time, does that mean I don't have any lovers soul agreements?

There are a variety of reasons a person may be without love relationships.

Though greatly enriching most people's lives, intimate relationships are not the path for every soul to achieve their current life goals. This category includes: the devoted nurse or nun who is spiritually elevated in her service to terminally ill children, the elderly man who finds purpose and joy tending to animals, the smiling Down's Syndrome child who people feel Divine love in the presence of, the wilderness guide who finds peace in the trees and the wind.

For those who are only temporarily alone, they may be developing their sense of independence and self-reliance first, and will hook up with their partner later in life.

Some people are alone because they are avoiding their soul agreements – they have been hurt and have not moved through the fear of failing again. Others might be taking an extended break from relationships after having gone through a series of growth and balancing agreements, and are just waiting for the right person. The question is "Do you want to be in a relationship, or not, and why."

If you are alone and desiring a love relationship, look at what may be holding you back. Do you need to clear your emotional patterns and fears? Are you keeping potential loves at a distance? What can you do to be more of your authentic self?

There has to be something better than all this relationship struggle!

The reward for your persistence moving through the soul growth and balancing agreements is arrival at the soulmate relationship.

What is a soulmate?

The soulmate agrees to provide love and support on a

---

long-term basis, to be the one who walks beside you as you embrace what your soul has come here to do in the world. Soulmates come together as equals with compatible goals, at a comparable level of development, with a deepening connection of trust and affection, to join energies for mutual success throughout life.

The potential is a love that surpasses the limitations of time and space, restoring awareness of your unity with all.

How does a soulmate agreement compare to other romantic relationships?

Where the earlier roles were often adversarial, with learning the hard way or in spite of, the role of the soulmate is to give their partner the emotional support and security needed to bloom and grow. Love relationships of soul growth or balancing may seem unfair, like a parasitic vine clinging to a tree for support, perhaps even choking the other's growth. In comparison, the soulmate agreement is two strong trees growing next to each other, both with their own network of sustaining roots and their branches intertwined as they reach for the sky.

When two souls agree to be soulmates, it is to be as equals, without the underlying loneliness or power struggles of soul balancing agreements. They are not drawn together to fill some lack or instill challenge, for they have already worked on their own soul growth. They are well matched, at a comparable level of emotional and intellectual capacity, with the same willingness and capacity to love.

Whereas the earlier relationships effectively point out your weaknesses and scarred places, the soulmate heart and soul connection is like looking in a mirror and seeing the beauty of your own being in the other. While maintaining healthy independence, the union of two in a soulmate relationship brings a sense that there is no "other," only wholeness. The focus is expansion rather than healing.

What does it take to make a soulmate agreement?

Such intimacy is only possible between two souls from the same soul family, with common roots and origins, (bringing a feeling of "home" when you reunite) and a history of relating through all kinds of agreements over the course of many lives.

You have been children, parents, and siblings to each other, as well as teachers, students, and friends, even adversaries, victims and abusers. With your most recent connections being benevolent close family or lovers, you pick up where you left off for the soulmate relationship. The exact number of lives together is less important than the quality and depth of previously established love and caring, proving you are trustworthy to unite so intimately.

Soulmates work best when there is comparable soul development and frame of reference. Unlike other soul

---

agreements where a difference in soul age is an asset for the lessons involved, soulmates connect best with the same level of experience. You will need equal standing as you move through life.

Do I only have one true soulmate?

No. If that were the case, the odds of actually finding that particular person would be so slim as to never happen. There are no guarantees, so you make enough agreements to ensure that no matter what happens in the world of chance and choice, a soulmate relationship will be possible for you.

While in the Spirit realm and designing your next Earth adventure, agreements are set up with perhaps three to thirty souls. "If our paths cross in this next life, I would attempt a soulmate relationship with you." Certain practical considerations – location, age, culture, gender, life-goals – all need to be compatible.

If one soul chooses to be born in the mountains of Russia and another born in urban Chicago, they would probably not meet, nor relate if they did. If one soul is going to be born in 1920 and the other isn't going to come in to their body until 1980, their age difference would make a soulmate agreement unworkable. (Especially when part of the agreement involves children.)

Radical differences in cultural background (racial, economic, or educational disparity) can make the chance of coming together and actualizing a soulmate relationship too remote to bother with. Gender choice is another factor to be considered. Are you looking to partner with a man or a woman this time? Equally important are personal path life goals. What are you coming here to do in the world? If you have a commitment to a life of service in impoverished regions, and your potential soulmate has a life task of accumulating great wealth, it may be too difficult for you to support each other's goals. Any soul agreement has to be compatible on the human level, here on Earth.

Much can happen between making the initial soulmate agreement in the Spirit realm and beginning love relationships as a teenager or young adult. The emotional maturity and skills your soul anticipates acquiring in childhood, and immediately after, is often different than what your human personality can accomplish. Unpredictable changes to the plan, such as a family moving, a parent dying, or a traumatic accident can radically impact the direction your life takes. One soul may transcend its unforeseen challenges while the other stays stuck in emotional struggles it thought would be easy, altering the soulmate compatibility.

Since life always involves unpredictable circumstances, soulmate agreements are formed with the understanding that if you meet in the coming life, and if you are still compatible, emotionally and intellectually, and if you are both still available, then you will attempt the soulmate relationship.

The reason for so many potentials is to cover all of the "ifs," so that you never run out of chances.

Are the agreements you make the same with each potential soulmate?

What they each agree to do for you is uniform, but what you agree to do for each of them will vary in accordance with their life goals. A woman sets up possibilities, first, with a potential soulmate who agrees to advance her as a leader through family connections in politics, while she agrees to help him become a musician. Her agreement with the second soul, who also agrees to assist with her leadership goal, is for her to support his career teaching disabled children.

Do people sometimes connect with more than one soulmate at a time?

On a soul level, soulmates watch for the availability of a prospective mate, and so it is not likely that two would present themselves at once. More often, when there are two strong relationship pulls, they are soul *growth* or *balancing* agreements that you mistake for a soulmate because of its intensity. When you are not able to let go of a soul agreement that isn't working or has been completed, a second love interest may provide extra motivation.

There are instances when there are two souls in your life at the same time with the feeling of soulmate – *the soulmate reminder agreement.*

What is a soulmate reminder agreement?

As a soul with particularly challenging lessons to over-come – you need someone who will be devoted to helping you shift, sticking with you until you do – you will make a special kind of soul growth agreement with a soul who was previously your soulmate.

Soulmate reminder agreements mimic the soulmate relationship in that both involve the unconditional love of a soul family member, a complex history of interaction and trust, and an intention to assist the other person in an important way.

The main difference is that the relationship is not designed to grow and evolve with increasing closeness, as a soulmate agreement does, but to last as long as the person needs such intense love and devotion to accomplish their lessons, with an eventual and graceful moving in their own direction.

The soulmate reminder agreement may take the form of lovers, or close family members such as parent or grand-parent and child, siblings, or twins. With lovers, the goal is to steer you into a fresh soulmate agreement. With family members, the promise is to give the unconditional love and support you need as you undergo tremendous challenge.

How do these soulmate reminder agreements work?

Two souls who have completed a successful and fulfilling soulmate agreement in a previous life, where tremendous love and devotion were established, can make an agreement to reunite when a temporary but profound heart and soul bond is required.

One example of a soulmate reminder relationship in a family setting is a mother with a handicapped child. The mother provides profound empathy and unconditional devotion, beyond the normal mothering, to support him in his particular challenges. There is a deep love and understanding shared, with the son having total faith that he will not be abandoned and the mother receiving a depth of connection that makes her sacrifices gratifying.

Eventually, as the son transcends his disability and launches himself into an empowered adult life, the importance of the mother/child bond lessens and the mother moves toward creating a new soulmate relationship with a lover.

The closeness of a soulmate reminder relationship between a parent and child can be hard for family members (particularly the parent's mate) who cannot compete with the closeness of these two. For a parent without a love partner, there is a risk of becoming emotionally attached and possessive which may interfere with the child's ability to develop independence.

Siblings also may form a soulmate reminder agreement, when those two souls are resistant to returning to the Earth journey without such a profound connection. If a soul is launching into a potentially difficult childhood, they'll need someone who knows them well, relates on a similar level, and will not abandon them – a previous soulmate can meet such a need. This is especially true with twins, who feel more confident and secure when there is another "just like me" (not only physically, but on a soul level) in the womb from the beginning. No matter how traumatic any other interaction may be, they will always have the unconditional love and trust of each other. That is, until they grow up and create their separate lives, and optimally, new soulmate relationships.

Lovers in a soulmate reminder agreement can mistakenly believe they are soulmates, because of their immediate sense of "I know and love you so deeply," but it is only a reminder. On a cellular level, coming together triggers soul memory vibrations of the previous soulmate union – ultimate love and trust. Presenting an example of profound soul connection combined with practical compatibility, this brief but powerful love shows you what you have been missing in your other unsuccessful relationships.

There is also usually some kind of built-in boundary that does not allow you to continue (drastic age difference, already married, distant location, etc.) which can cause frustration and heartache. The passion stirred up in a soul-mate reminder encounter creates a powerful longing for the unconditional love of a soulmate, shows that it is possible, and makes you acutely aware of what not to do *without* in a relationship.

Even though you may be reluctant to let go, trust that the beauty and purpose of this soulmate reminder is to lead you to "the real thing."

Are soulmate relationships always successful in the long term?

There are no guarantees of success in any soul agreement, just a preliminary promise to try. There may be intense love and attraction, and a feeling of profound soul union, but unless both are totally capable of unconditional love, and devoted to encouraging the life goals of the other, there will be more frustration than comfort or bliss.

The level of success will be by degree. The more personal growth that has been accomplished, the more the magic of the soulmate synergy can flow, shining out to the world and bringing in miracles and empowering shifts for both.

The introduction of a soulmate does not "cure the pain" or eliminate problems, but gives a person greater emotional resources. The intention is that each person will have unconditional love and support as they tackle their own challenges. If a soulmate connection happens before either has worked on the lessons of wisdom and emotional strength through earlier relationships of struggle, they may not be capable of embracing what the soulmate relationship offers.

An example would be a young soulmate couple that had just begun to unravel and understand the programming and hardships of their childhoods. When they met right after high school, there was an incredible sense of companionship and understanding, with an unspoken hope that such love could "save" them. As in the story of "The Ugly Duckling," they felt like they had finally met another beautiful swan instead of being told by the ducks that there was something wrong with them!

Because she had not worked through issues of disempowerment, and he had not addressed his need to control, they were too extreme in their own imbalances to be able to interact without conflict. Actually, the soulmate relationship began to take on qualities of a soul growth agreement – struggle and heartache. Although there always was support and love, their immature emotions and actions led them to blame, frustration, and separation.

Had they each been aware of their need to face their own issues, they might have been able to move through tough times and evolve to a purer soulmate connection.

What happens when one of the soulmates is ready, but the other has much work left to do?

A soulmate agreement is made in the Spirit realm as both souls are reviewing their intended plans for childhood lessons and environments. Perhaps they both set up lives with parents who are to provide emotional stability and a college education, anticipating a certain level of development, and arranging a soulmate agreement with each other as they will be equally advanced.

As a result of chance, a parent of the first soul dies, greatly altering life circumstances and causing him to face the unforeseen issues of abandonment and financial hardship. Growing into adulthood with extremely different attitudes and qualities than expected, the difficulties encountered may set the first soul back to the point where the two souls are at totally different levels. When they meet, they are still drawn together, but their initial agreement is no longer compatible or workable.

The first soul may feel unworthy or resist the connection, expect the other to take care of him, or unconsciously sabotage the relationship with infidelity, neglect or conflict. The second soul, expecting an equal, may become highly critical. She may push for "catch-up" growth or try to "rescue" the first soul, making extreme concessions for his shortcomings or tolerating unacceptable treatment.

Even without a turn of events, there are cases where one person has not done their necessary growth – perhaps escaping into drugs or alcohol or blaming others. When they meet their soulmate, their unresolved problems become more apparent as the soulmate energy shines a light on any shadow self. Even with their partner's love and support, there may still be resistance to change and an increase of avoidance behaviors. "I won't grow up and you can't make me!"

How do you tell the difference between a soul growth agreement and a soulmate agreement that's not working?

If you are in a soulmate relationship that is not working, when disagreements surface, the emotional pain you experience can feel more like the soul growth relationship. Discord and conflict in a soulmate relationship arises from an underlying sense of being tricked or misled – "You're not the soulmate you said you would be" – rather than your unresolved issues coming up to be healed in a growth agreement – "I'm getting stronger every time you push me."

When you feel your buttons getting pushed, ask yourself, "What is the true source of my pain?" and "Is my partner challenging me or supporting me?" If you feel alone even though you are in a relationship, it is probably the growth kind. If you feel safe enough to address the issues that are coming up without fear of losing love, you are probably in a soulmate relationship, even if you are mismatched.

How do you know when it is appropriate to bail on a soulmate relationship?

It is the same for any relationship, soulmate or otherwise. Look at the proportion of effort to pay off.

Is the overall quality of the relationship worth the low points? Are the problems temporary or ongoing, decreasing in intensity or getting worse than ever? Do you support each other or hurt each other?

Is the love you are giving equal to the amount you are receiving? Is your heart connection still flowing both ways, or does it feels unsafe?

Are you really compatible or is it a mismatch that you are trying to force? How long have you been trying without improvement, and is it all up to you or is the other willing to do their part?

Are one person's unaddressed personal problems getting in the way of healthy relating? Are misunderstandings caused by unclear communication or assumptions? Are you venting in panic instead of expressing authentic feelings?

After a fight, is the problem really solved, or are you just giving up in exhaustion and futility because your differences are unchangeable?

Remember, this is not the only chance for love.

Your soul has made enough potential soulmates to ensure that if you let this relationship go, there can be another. And the same is true for the one you are leaving. They would be better off with a soul that matches who they are now, instead of trying to fulfill your impossible requirements!

If one relationship does not work, graciously move on to the next. Neither of you will run out of chances for love.

Why is it so hard to end a relationship?

People get confused about the difference between loving their partner's soul potential and putting up with incompatible traits and behaviors. Even with the greatest intentions, the human personality simply may not be capable of being or doing what the soul has hoped for.

You do not have to determine that someone was bad, wrong, or evil. You do not have to create huge drama or conflict – some people can only leave when attraction turns to hate or blame. You do not have to give up loving their soul essence, but understand that who they are right now is not a good fit with who you are right now. Love their soul, bless them for trying, at whatever level they were able, and set them free. Both they, and you, deserve to love again.

What about when a soulmate dies? What happens to the other partner?

Though the emotional trauma and incredible sense of loss can be overwhelming, the challenge is to continue to feel soulmate love, even though that specific person is no longer with you in a physical way.

What happens to the partner depends on the ages of

those involved, whether the soulmate relationship was working well or not, and the attitude of the one still living.

When an older person's soulmate dies, it is not unusual for the other to die soon after. With such a strong life-long bond, there can be a pull from the other side, with encouragement to let go of attachment to Earth and move on to the Spirit realm. Or the other may live many more years, sustained with an unseen connection and the memory of true love worn like a comforting cloak.

When a younger person's soulmate dies, the situation becomes more like soulmates that do not fulfill the agreement. There are still opportunities for other soulmates, others who would bring the same powerful feeling of "home." The one you have lost is only one of many who have agreed to share love with you in this way.

The first example is a woman who was in a beautifully connected soulmate partnership. Her husband died in an accident when their son was only seven. She was so committed to him in her heart and soul devotion, and could not see dating as anything but "unfaithful" to him, that she endured ten years of isolation in grief and abandonment. It was only when she was able to understand that his wish for her would be to love and be loved, that she was able to release her first soulmate and seek another.

The second example is a man whose soulmate connection

was filled with emotional turmoil as his wife was stuck in personal suffering and had turned to drugs to ease her pain. As a result, when she died of an overdose, his sense of responsibility for having failed her was added to the emotional trauma of being abandoned by his soulmate. Coming to realize that her departure was not to be taken personally (it had nothing to do with their love or soul connection), he was able to see that her soul had taken on more than she could handle. With restored compassion, he began to embrace the possibility of meeting another soulmate, this time with one who was less damaged and more able to connect with him as an equal for a fulfilling relationship.

Be attentive to healing the emotional pain that can result from such a devastating loss, otherwise you may fall into a less than desirable relationship inspired not by an authentic bond, but a severe need to fill the void in your heart.

When you lose love, instead of being swallowed in grief, anger, or self-pity, say, "Wow! I had a taste of what it's all about!" "Now I know what to look for in a relationship." With the attitude of a child finishing an exquisitely flavored ice cream cone, rejoice in the sensation (even though this one's finished) and look forward to the next!

How do I attract a soulmate into my life?

Before you focus on bringing in a soulmate, there are three questions to ask yourself.

1. Have you addressed the emotional fears and behavior patterns that occurred in your other love relationships, or are you hoping that the perfect person will fix your problems?

2. Do you present your authentic self to the world, or do you modify your goals, behavior, and essence for approval?

3. Are you embracing the path that brings you inspiration, purpose, and contentment, or are you avoiding it or waiting for a soulmate to create it for you?

Number one: Deal with your own emotional pain to the greatest level that you are able. Embracing your healing means boldly revealing your weaknesses and doing whatever it takes to get stronger and more in balance. If you haven't dealt with previous pain, you are as the walking wounded and more likely to draw in a soul growth agreement than a soulmate.

When desperate longing does attract a soulmate, the result is a relationship where one soulmate is needy and the other is not ready. "My soulmate is in so much pain. I am not healed enough yet, but I'll be with her anyway." Chances are the relationship will be filled with trouble and disappointment, the work still to be done taking all the fun out of the soulmate relationship.

Number two: Be mindful of the image you project. If you are not authentic, you will attract someone who is looking for someone else. Your true soulmate is looking for your true self. How do you think they will recognize you if you are wearing a disguise? There is an analogy: Perhaps you began life, your soul shining with a bright yellow light, but you quickly discovered that you only received love and acceptance if you dimmed down that light and changed your glow to a light blue. As you go through life, you attract those seeking light blue partners, and those whose job it is to help (or force) you to switch back to bright yellow. It is only when you are shining with your true radiance that your matching yellow beacon will find you.

Number three: Since the soulmate agreement relates to your greater role in the world, embarking on your soul purpose brings a greater chance of meeting your soulmate. The soulmate agreement involves supporting you on that path, but they are not responsible to get you started. What could you do with your life if nothing stopped you? Explore the possibilities and you get a few steps closer.

Look back at your childhood, to activities and ways of relating that were natural and fulfilling. Did helping old people make your heart shine? Did dismantling and reassembling the toaster fill you with inspiration? Did playing an instrument take you far beyond yourself? What makes you feel empowered and glad to be alive?

If you wish for a soulmate to rescue you from your life, you may wait a long time. The irony is that they are more likely to come along when you have already taken care of it yourself!

What are twin flames? Are they like soulmates, or
are they two separated parts of the same soul?

Also called task companions, the twin flame is the best friend who sees you through your tough times, but without the romantic involvement of the soulmate. They understand what you are going through, and assist, without being enmeshed in your situation. Sharing the same types of trials and challenging encounters, twin flames take turns being support on a parallel path of learning. You may have more than one twin flame, meeting up with one, and then another, as life challenges change.

It is a romantic notion that you may have a lost aspect of your soul and finally be made whole again by finding it in another person. If your soul could split in two (which would serve no purpose, and which it will not), the chances of reuniting would be remote. A soulmate union might feel like you have joined your missing half, but each person has their own individualized essence.

How does the soul age relate to the kinds of rela-
tionships a person attracts?

Younger souls mainly focus on soul growth and balancing agreements to accumulate experience through many interactions, as they develop the self-sufficiency, emotional maturity, and wisdom required to have a successful soulmate relationship later. There is value in every attempt – to try something and not be successful teaches what not to do. The soulmate agreement is something that a soul works up to as their love relationships become more sophisticated through the course of many lives.

All soul agreements and relationships, including the soulmate, are directly related to what you are trying to accomplish on a soul level. What you need to undo from the past and what you are here to do in the world points your soul in the direction of your most purposeful relationships.

The following example is a simplified tracing of one soul through many lives:

The soul begins its incarnations in a primitive clan setting; a select focus on agreements with core soul family members. In the earliest lives, learning how to survive is the primary task, so the soul's agreement for a mate is based on the physical needs of protection, food, warmth, and breeding rather than emotional fulfillment.

As the soul evolves, interactions and agreements expand to those outside the immediate community. In this life, as a man, he negotiates a marriage to a woman from a neighboring village. Theirs is a practical union, with the soul task of embracing the beginnings of emotional connection. He does not care for her, but instead, is unsympathetic and controlling while he endures the commitment.

The next lifetime, the soul is a woman, with the goal of

understanding what it is like to be unloved. The perfect scenario will be to arrange a soul balancing agreement with the soul who was previously the wife, to swap roles. Throughout her life, she endures poor treatment without emotional connection or support, and learns the importance of love and compassion.

During the stage of a young soul where the challenge of competition is explored, the soul makes agreements to fight over a mate. To have the soul experience of getting his way no matter what, he falls in love with a woman betrothed to another man, and wins her hand in a duel to the death. The next life fulfills that soul's need for balancing with an agreement for an intensely passionate encounter with that same soul (the woman), but this time she is already married and he cannot have her. He is resigned to marry another, as an opportunity to overcome his earlier frustration in love. Learning to cope with not getting his way – he may chose violent revenge or acceptance – is the main soul task in that life.

Emotional satisfaction and the ability to relate become more important as a soul develops. The soul, this time a woman, makes a number of agreements for the possibility of several mates within the span of one life. She takes on the opportunity to improve how she relates in an accelerated fashion. Her first husband is a controlling brute, a soul growth agreement pushing her to be emotionally self-reliant and stand up for herself. Her second husband is meek and undirected, a soul balancing agreement to show her the opposite – safety, but no passion – which she responds to with hostility and impatience. Her third husband is her first attempt at a soulmate agreement. They come together with intense love, but are so inexperienced at harmonious relating, with their old fears and patterns, that the relationship is filled with emotional chaos and thwarted expectations. She learns what a soulmate feels like, but is not yet prepared enough in her own personal growth for a soulmate to bring exalted union.

After multiple lives and a variety of partnerships – some soul agreements of growth or balancing, others as unsuccessful attempts at soulmate relationships – the soul has gained valuable experience in love partnerships. As an older soul, there is an intention to fulfill a soulmate relationship, but also the desire to embrace the soul's work in the world – expressing the beauty of the sublime through music. Coming into a male body this time, the soul sets up agreements for his childhood training, as well as the growth and balancing agreements that will prepare him for a soulmate, of which there are eighteen potential souls.

His childhood environment affords him encouragement in his musical talents, but his first relationship is with a woman whose need for financial security distracts him and he gives up his dreams of being a musician (a soul growth challenge). Learning how important musical passion is to his happiness, he ends the relationship. Next, he finds a soulmate who is encouraging and supportive of him being a musician, but her unfaithfulness and dependency on drugs (resulting from an unexpectedly destructive and unhealed childhood), interferes with his career and destroys the relationship. Determined not to give up his soul purpose, he wrenches himself from a painful soulmate separation and sense of failure, and moves on.

He goes through a series of soul growth and balancing relationships to gain strength and self-love, to end a cycle of choosing partners he must appease. At one point in his journey, he falls in love with a woman who is everything he ever wanted, but she is married to someone else. Even though the relationship cannot be actualized, he now grasps what it is to feel real unconditional love. This soulmate reminder agreement shows him the depth of connection and qualities that were missing from his other relationships.

Setting aside his longing to be in relationship, he shifts his focus towards his life goals of music. When he next encounters love, she is a soulmate who has a similar story of misadventures and personal growth. They are each now able to embrace the soulmate partnership in a healthy way, without giving up goals. She is strong enough in her own life passions and emotional self-sufficiency to be able to help him achieve his dreams while attaining her own. It works both ways, as they celebrate their successes together. His soul has finally achieved a fulfilling soulmate relationship in alignment with accomplishment of his life task.

In a following life, this soul chooses to attempt a different life purpose, and in order to do so, needs the support of an extraordinary soul. So he chooses to form an agreement with the one who was previously his soulmate, to now be a sibling.

On and on... Like waves on a beach in a continual over-lapping flow, the cycle of lives progresses. With each attempt, there is learning, and there are endless opportunities to try again. Through each fulfilling soulmate relationship, the soul is creating evolved and enduring bonds with others in the soul family. In future lives, their interactions will be mutually advantagous, harmonious and bring greater levels of love and accomplishment.

For some soulmates, part of their life purpose is to work through all of the relationship struggles, culminating in a joyful soulmate partnership to be an example to the world of what is possible. With deep appreciation and gratitude, they serve as inspiration and hope to those who are longing for such a love. There is a benefit for the whole human race when soulmate couples are able to express and spread their vibration of love and joy. Who would you rather be around, a couple who are stirring up each other's fears or a couple who adore and bring out the best in each other?

With successful soulmates, what happens after that lifetime? Do they come back together as soulmates again?

Once you have completed an agreement with one soul, you are more likely to embrace a new soulmate relationship with someone else rather than repeating the same experience. The situation that does bring two soulmates back together again is when they were not able to fulfill the relationship previously. If one or the other was not individually prepared to embrace their agreement and they separated, or if one died before they could reach the level of union they desired, they may make another agreement to try again. This is often the case with couples that come together when very young as high school sweethearts. They had already started a connection, and now are picking up where they left off, without needing to go through a series of soul growth agreements.

Two successful soulmates may also decide to continue an interaction of great love and trust, but not as soulmates. They may return in another life as siblings, parent and child, or lovers – the soulmate reminder agreement. Devoted to each other, but not intertwined in the same way.

From the standpoint of human emotion, it may sound desirable to remain in the bliss and safety of one successful soulmate encounter, but not from the soul perspective. The goal is always to try something new, to have loving connections with many souls, to expand and grow. For it is through multiple successful soulmate relationships that a soul evolves by leaps and bounds.

The lovers agreements are an attempt to experience soul comfort and belonging on a physical plane level, to bring the essence of sublime spiritual union into the current life reality. It is beautiful to feel and be reminded, through the love of another person, that you are valuable, and that you are not alone here.

YOUR SPIRIT TEAM

Your soul path is a team effort.

You are not meant to go through life feeling lonely or separate, or to be limited in what you can accomplish. There are other people to share your experiences, as well as soul family members on the other side and Spirit guides to help you. Spirit guides are like "wind in your sails," giving you an extra push and making your journey easier. Among all of the souls who are Spirit guides, there is a dedicated group who are especially connected to you – your *personal* Spirit Team.

Who are these Spirit Team helpers?

There are a select few from among your soul family Spirit guides (those who have gone through all of their cycle of lives and are now assisting others) who have made a specific and powerful soul agreement with you for this life.

Their agreement is to make sure you feel loved and connected, to assist you in accomplishing your tasks and to remind you of your exalted soul essence. *Your* agreement is to let them.

You are part of a team – an Earth mission team – and you are the emissary who is in a physical body while your Spirit Team operates from the Spirit realm. You are the one who is capable of tangible movement and choices while they, having recently mastered the challenges of a series of Earth lives, are now able to operate as multidimensional, magical beings.

The "mission" of your Spirit Team is to serve as back up support as you live your life on Earth. Without their participation, your soul tasks and human experiences are more of a struggle. Without your cooperation, your Spirit Team cannot fulfill their part of your soul agreement and cannot achieve *their* next level of soul growth.

What is the difference between Spirit Team guides and our soul family members that are between lives?

Like all other soul family members with whom you make agreements, you have shared many lifetimes and a wide variety of relationships and experiences. Both Spirit Team guides and soul family members between lives can show up as wise guides to provide loving comfort and strong protection, as well as to serve as a prodding nemesis or a tough-love teacher.

The ones who are between lives are like the grandmother who passes on, and yet, you feel her presence and may even hear her words of love and wisdom on occasion – a soul agreement with a bond continuing beyond her death. There is still a link to the personality of that life and their relationship to you in your present form. They will continue to have the "appearance" and characteristics of the person they were in physical form, while Spirit Team guides present themselves with whatever archetypal imagery fits your frame of reference.

The soul agreement between you and your Spirit Team is arranged prior to your birth with a unified plan for a group goal. If your soul purpose is to become a leader for change, *their* purpose is to help you become that leader in an exalted way. Your Spirit Team has a singular focus that matches yours – their only agenda is to help you succeed – while souls that are still incarnating have complex agreements and tasks. The grandmother on the other side, for instance, may have one agreement with you to provide the nurturing you did not receive from mother, while she is making agreements for her next life involving a difficult husband to compel her to gain strength, and a soul task of overcoming poverty.

For those between lives, there is much healing and learning left to do. In comparison, your Spirit Team has transcended the dynamics of relationship struggles. They are not influenced by your choices and have no individual needs to be met. They are not subject to emotions, personality flaws, judgments, or agendas, but they still have awareness and compassion of how difficult life can be, from their own recent human experiences.

How does our Spirit Team interact with us?

With perfect wisdom and unconditional love, sometimes waiting and watching, sometimes interjecting and influencing, these special guides show up at different times in your life, whenever their particular function is most important for you.

Each person has at least six guides on their Spirit Team that fall into archetypal roles, similar for everyone. This system of helpers can be thought of like a group of employees hired for a project, each offering their unique skills for a particular task. It is not appropriate for you to do their job or to try and handle the whole project single-handedly. The project is your soul purpose. Your job is to move about in the physical world, actualizing choices. Their job is to do what you cannot, create miracles.

What are the six roles of the Spirit Team?

They are best described as the state of being opposite to the human challenge that they assist with.

Fear: The Nurturer comforts in times of fear, loneliness, and low self-worth.

Chaos: The Wise Protector, the one who pulls you out of confusion or danger.

Lack: The Treasurer provides material goods necessary to survive and thrive.

Disease: The Body Healer insures that your Earth Suit functions well.

Separation: The Networker hooks you up with human helpers and companions.

Stagnation: The Creative Muse with the infusion of fresh ideas and spontaneity.

How do these six guides help us?

The Nurturer: As an archetype of Divine Mother, this is the one who soothes and nurtures, and through whose presence, a person remembers and retains the sense of unconditional love and acceptance that a soul easily embraces in the Spirit realm. The one who helps you feel comfortable being here. This is valuable as an avenue to experience *receiving* love, especially when people in your life are not available or capable of loving the way every person deserves to be loved. Often, your Nurturer can fill the gap left by one's own mother, who was after all, only human.

The Wise Protector: As an archetype of Divine Father, the one who keeps you safe and shares knowledge. The teacher, the guide to knowing who to trust and not to trust, how it works here in this world, and which choices are best for you. This is the one to provide sage wisdom as well as security in the physical world. Sometimes, your Wise Protector steers you away from harm while other times providing an intense challenge or wake-up call when needed. This guide keeps you going in the right direction, whether you like it or not! It is helpful to focus on your Wise Protector, especially when your father was absent, or lacking of these qualities.

The Treasurer: For every time that you have done the right thing instead of the easy thing, energy – like an amount of money – has been deposited in your soul bank account. Accumulating through all of your lives, there is now abundance available to you as you embark on your soul's journey. Your Treasurer serves as the banker who sends exactly what you need – the money, the supplies, the opportunities for work. You are merely "withdrawing" resources that you have previously earned. Your Treasurer will not respond to demands for funds that fuel greed, ego, selfishness, or power but will always support your soul purpose.

The Body Healer: The Body Healer is devoted to helping maintain your body free of pain, disability, and disease, but may accentuate sensations or difficulties in various areas to get you to pay attention to what you are neglecting.

There is an association with the DNA soul memories

held in the body, in that this Spirit Team guide has full awareness and knowledge of your predispositions towards ailments and what your soul needs to learn and release for the body. Your Body Healer has ultimate wisdom about your particular diet, exercise, and remedy needs.

The Networker: There are many people involved in the tasks of your soul purpose. In order to make sure that you connect with the right ones – those you have agreements with – your Networker has instant access and ability to send them your way. Chance meetings with vital people may be appointments set by this member of your Spirit Team. Your Networker also sends the appropriate person to teach you a lesson or provide an example when you need it.

The Creative Muse: Without this guide, you might become too serious or rigid, fixed in the responsibilities of life and the patterns of what has come before. This is the Spirit Team member who brings inspiration, playfulness, spontaneity, and gives you the courage to take risks. Your Creative Muse leads you to which color to paint next, the perfect note to add to a harmony, or the idea that creates a brilliant invention. When you call this one in, there is an infused energy and spirit of adventure added to life. When you ignore it, your Creative Muse may show up to play tricks on you to get your attention and remind you of what is missing.

I have real people in my life who fill these roles. Do I still need my Spirit Team?

Not to diminish their importance, but the people in your life serve as the temporary vehicle for these archetypal energies to act through. People can come and go in your life, but your Spirit Team is available at any time and for the duration of your life. If you have been receiving money through a father or a boss, understand that they are not the source. If their soul agreement to provide you with money ends, your Treasurer will find another way to sustain you on your path.

If my Spirit Team is always there for me, are they dedicated only to me?

Each Spirit Team group is part of the Universal Soul, more individuated than the collective mass, but more inter-connected than humans who are still in bodies. They are not limited by the confines of human bodies nor time and space constraints.

They can be part of more than one team, simultaneously assisting and interacting with you as well as other people. This multilevel functioning does not limit their ability or their connection to you in any way.

I don't feel or experience a Spirit Team. Are you sure I have one?

The separation that people sometimes feel is only a

result of being encased in these physical forms, and believing that you are separate.

You have agreements whether you are aware of these guides or not. They can give more effective assistance when you actively participate and call them in. Then they don't have to "whack" you to get your attention. Instead, you will have instant access to their magic.

Realigning with your Spirit Team gives you the ability to shift into more powerful and successful ways of being to a huge degree.

How do I know who my Spirit Team is?

Your Spirit Team may not be apparent or obvious in any tangible way, as with seeing a person standing in front of you or hearing someone talking, and it is not terribly important that you have a specific description of them. Gathering impressions about a name, a characterization, and a purpose may be useful in helping you focus on them, and in believing that they exist, but it is not important for such an identification to be *real*, in the sense that you are accustomed to.

There have already been times when they have made their subtle presence known. Your Spirit Team guide may show up in a dream in the form of a stranger approaching to give you a warning or piece of advice, or a strong soldier beside you as you walk down a dark street. In your waking world, there are times when just thinking about something you need calls them in. "I wonder where I'm going to get a new washing machine," will be heard without any kind of acknowledgment, and within a few days, a friend tells you that they have a really nice one they don't need.

You do not have to have any special gifts or clairvoyant abilities to connect to your Spirit Team, just a strong desire and an open mind. The best way to find out more about your Spirit Team is to step out of your customary expectations, and shift from having to "know" who they are or what is happening. As you begin to use your imagination, and trust that they exist, you can begin to "play" with all of this, and see what happens.

How do I work with my team?

What this requires is a break from frenetic "doing," a little bit of trusting instead of controlling and allowing instead of demanding. Play with the idea that they *do* exist, that they *can* hear you, and that you *can* ask for what you need. Take a moment to set aside the usual way you try and make things happen. Pay attention to what you might be able to sense and feel beyond your conscious mind. Know that there is *something* that you can reach out to and draw in, and be willing to expose yourself to unseen possibility.

Move beyond any thoughts that you are not worthy or should not ask for help. Let go of thinking that you should control the next move, or that you even could. Step aside and allow your Spirit Team to do their job. *Your* new job is "Receiving."

A great example of how my Spirit Team worked with me was the time I needed a place to live. After plowing through the want ads, I became discouraged by the high cost and low quality of rentals available. So I turned to visioning, creating a list of everything included in my perfect dream home. Nothing precise such as "two bedrooms," but rather, "plenty of room for living, playing, and working." Instead of "$800/month" I wrote, "affordable." I set the list aside, and imaged being in a place fitting my description. It *felt* good and I began to have faith that such a home existed.

I stated my need to my Spirit Team, and I opened to their guidance, by asking, "Send me where I need to be next." For some reason (influence of my Creative Muse?), I was inspired to actually draw a rough sketch of a home, bringing the image even more present in the realm of possibilities. The next day, I awoke from a dream with the words, "Go to the Salem Unity," sounding in my mind (perhaps a message from my Networker). I believed that I was being led to check out the church, and approached a woman after the service who responded to my introduction by asking with excitement, "You wouldn't be looking for a house to rent, would you?" The house was exactly as I had drawn it! Though much larger, more beautiful, and less expensive than

I expected (thank you, Treasurer), it was perfect. Even the arrangements with the landlords were generous and smooth. As it turned out, living in this house actually brought an abundance of clients, through my association with the Unity folks. My Spirit Team had led me to the perfect manifestation of my every need, beyond my greatest expectations.

Is there a way for me *to make this connection happen?*

It is your clarity of intention that sets things in motion, your desire to open to connection and assistance that invites their participation. Creating an image in your mind – a symbolic persona – helps your connection be consistent and strong. With the knowledge that your Spirit Team will show up in a way that fits your frame of reference, open to seeing and feeling the presence, including a name, a bodily appearance with gender and costume, assigning some characteristic qualities that fit what you need them to be. (Gender is less important than the qualities they embody). Whatever image shows up in your mind is exactly perfect for you.

For **The Nurturer**, bring forth an image that makes you feel comfortable and loved, perhaps an angel dressed in white, or a beautiful Greek Goddess. Perhaps she is a roly-poly country Grandma wearing a checkered dress, or an elegant fairy-tale queen, or a soft mama bird.

For **The Wise Protector,** imagine an archetype of

strength and wisdom that you can totally trust to take care of you. Perhaps he is a warrior king of old, or an ancient sage with infinite wisdom. Whatever works for you – a powerful but peaceful guardian, policeman, computer android, or strong papa bear – who makes you feel safe and secure.

For **The Treasurer,** create a visual definition of a benefactor, a generous wise distributor of your funds. This could be a banker behind a desk, Cinderella's Fairy God-mother, a magician with gold and jewels, or the warehouse officer in charge of distributing supplies. Picture yourself receiving, from whomever is freely handing you what you need.

For **The Body Healer,** there is a blending of ancient wisdom with modern medical knowledge, a quality of com-passionate attention combined with tough love. Your image could be a hospital nurse, an ancient mystical healer, a native shaman medicine man, or a superhero with powers to heal. You could imagine a mechanic, fine tuning and repairing your body as if it were a valuable precision machine.

For **The Networker,** picture someone who is able to attract, select, and connect you to the perfect person you need for the next step. This could be the secretary of human resources in a large corporation, a switchboard telephone operator, the Town Crier, or a hotel lobby clerk checking in guests and relaying messages.

For **The Creative Muse,** imagine someone playfully making you laugh, delighting you with new ideas. This archetypal image could show up as a tinker-bell fairy, a Vaudeville performer, or an elaborately dressed elf. Perhaps it is a jovial old wizard, or a grandmotherly figure with a mischievous twinkle in her eye.

There is no universal image, no set "persona" for Spirit Team guides. People have previous associations and frames of reference. An archetype that works for one person might have no meaning for another, and some people have had negative experiences that require them to be especially creative in their imagery. A woman had a mother who was severely disturbed and abusive, making it too difficult for her to feel safe with *any* kind of human female figure, so her Nurturer came to her in the form of a giant white mother bird. With this non-human image, she could trust the love and comfort offered her as she imagined being wrapped in luxurious feather wings. A woman who felt intimidated by men needed an extra strong archetype to help her feel protected and have trust in solid wisdom, so her Wise Protector took on the form of an ancient Celtic Warrior woman. A man who had very stern and serious associations concerning hard work and money could only accept receiving from his Treasurer through an image of a boss paying him for work he had done in the past.

It does not matter what they look like or if your imagery

makes sense to anyone else. It does not matter what you call them, it is only important that you do.

How do I know that what I am connecting to is healthy? Maybe it's a ghost.

Ghosts make their presence known through the emotions, by projecting whatever state they were experiencing at death – fear, anger, sadness – onto you. They get your attention by making *you* feel what they *feel*. Spirit guides do not impose themselves in an obsessive way, nor do they make you feel worse.

Ghosts are crying for help, whereas those of the Spirit Team cry, "Let me help!"

Why do we resist having such help?

From your experience with people – being let down, controlled, or distracted from your own needs – you are now suspicious of any kind of partnership, even when a beneficial option presents itself.

Are you afraid of someone controlling you? Your Spirit Team will never impose a directive and have no goals other than your success.

Used to others disappointing you, asking and not receiving? Your guides are masterful and dependable, though they will not assist you in going the wrong direction.

Do you need to prove that you are self-reliant? Your

Spirit Team will *insist* you do your part. They provide only backup and support as you take care of the activities of the physical plane.

Will there be a price to pay for their help? Those on your Spirit Team do not want anything from you, other than that they achieve their goal – assisting you.

See your connection to these special guides as different than your human experiences, and move past your natural inclination to retreat into what you are used to – doing it all yourself. Self-sufficiency is important, but so is working as a team, and recognizing the power in numbers.

Play with the idea that your team is thrilled to be helping you, with no strings attached, and with the outcome of miracles. *Pretend* that this is so, practicing acceptance of that idea, until it becomes comfortable and familiar.

Why should I give up being in control of my own life?

It is never healthy for you to stop being in charge of your own choices.

The style of their guidance is not so much in the form of instructions or orders, it is as assurance, giving you confidence that what you were already inspired to do is the right thing. It's not like you need someone to tell you what to do, but the support of your Spirit Team creates a feeling of trusting yourself rather than the insecurity of confusion or indecision.

Do these guides help us even when we don't embrace this connection?

Sometimes it is a gentle guiding, behind the scenes, effective even when we are not aware. Like the time you feel the steering wheel turn you away from an accident with oncoming traffic, just in time. An unexpected check comes in the mail right when you need it most. Or a helpful person shows up to guide you when you are lost in a foreign country. Other times, it's not so easy or pleasant.

"We've been watching this soul struggle and insist on doing everything herself, the hard way. We see that life hasn't been easy and she doesn't know how to reach out to us. We can no longer wait patiently as this soul continues down the wrong path, alone in pain and frustration."

Time for the cosmic two-by-four – the message that cannot be ignored. Being fired from your job when you have been totally miserable, but too afraid to quit. Having an accident or injury that forces you to reevaluate your actions. Both circumstances open you to the idea of seeking new insights and options, a perfect time to begin listening, and asking for help from your team.

Can I just ask for anything and my Spirit Team will grant it?

If your request serves your higher good, then yes. If your desire is based on human needs and fears, no. You can be driven by ideas that are not really good for you, as you try to solve problems from the limited perspective of human life, but your team remains focused on what you *actually* need.

"I am open to having a really good, loving relationship," works better than, "I want Mary to be madly in love with me."

"I am open to receiving the perfect form of transportation," will bring a better solution than "ordering" a new red sports car.

Have you ever tried to make something happen that you were not supposed to get? Push though you might, everything is hard, goes wrong, and falls through.

The universe does not respond to impositions of your will, but when you align with your higher soul purpose, which includes cooperating with your Spirit Team, the universe rewards you.

With the essence of your Spirit Team present in your mind, you bring about a shift. It is as if your attention *to* them results in attention *from* them. Little messages begin to permeate your thoughts. You find yourself being led to good ideas, wise moves, lucky breaks, and serendipitous meetings.

Instead of feeling like a blind-folded person, stumbling through a hedge maze, you have helpers looking out over the whole picture and guiding you in the game, "Left here, now straight ahead. That's right. Keep going."

SOUL PURPOSE

Your true nature is to follow your soul path.

How do I know what my soul purpose is?

From the time you began your human life, your soul was intent on embracing the soul purpose. However, you first had to focus on the challenge of your childhood training and the soul growth and balancing that needed to be addressed. So, by the time you are ready for your soul path, you may have forgotten what it is.

Often times, you can look back to your early childhood for clues to what you enjoyed doing naturally, before people told you what you *should* do, or you began responding to human fears or responsibilities. What was it that made you feel glad to be alive?

Perhaps you don't remember much from your childhood, so what kinds of things do you automatically do now that make you feel a rightness of being? Do you feel good when you are helping someone? Creating? Entertaining? Taking charge? Organizing?

When you watch a movie or read a book, what kind of person do you identify with or wish you could be more like? Would you like to be defending the powerless? Exploring? or simply playing?

What kinds of soul path do people have?

There are teachers, artists, prophets, and entertainers; warriors, inventors, scholars and storytellers; entrepreneurs, negotiators, adventurers; builders, healers, athletes, and leaders. No path is greater than another, for you will explore each of them over the course of all your lives.

The soul may chose to be of great service to the world, or take on a personal challenge. There are noble goals to improve the quality of water, to bring joy to children in a cancer ward, or to overthrow a brutal dictator. Others may focus on improving the financial and educational status of their family, being the devoted helpmate to someone else, or living a peaceful existence in solitude and reflection.

Sometimes through *doing*, sometimes through *being*, the soul path could be achieved by inventing and implementing a new system of communication, or living as an open-hearted handicapped child setting an example of unconditional love. No soul purpose should be judged as less important, for even a path of *enjoying* is valuable, especially to show others how good life can be.

Does my soul purpose have to match what I do for a living?

The soul path does not need to be accomplished through a tangible career or in a gigantic way. For some, the soul purpose "leadership" is fulfilled through the roll of president of a nation. Other leaders need only take charge of steering their children out of chaos into successful lives.

Your soul could take on the task of agitating, of stirring people up when they are complacent, of shaking up the systems that have become rigid or out of balance. Your purpose could be to smooth, soothe and calm that which is frenetic or chaotic, or your soul path could involve maintaining a neutral stance in all things.

The goal is to fully embrace *who* you are and *how* you are to be in this life. Then, whatever your soul's mission, you will gravitate to where you can express your path in a tangible way. If your soul purpose is "to smooth," *be that* out in the world. "Smooth" as you drive around in traffic. "Smooth" as you tend to children. "Smooth" as you stand in line at the bank. You can be successful in your soul path even though you will not find a job in the want ads for a "Smoother."

Can a person have more than one soul purpose?

There is usually just one general direction, but the avenues of expression and fulfillment can vary. The "smoother" may find a unique niche for that way of being, perhaps as a diplomatic or corporate mediator.

If your soul purpose is to teach other people how to achieve their full potential, your first "assignment" could be in your role as a parent, being that teacher for your children. Later, that path may manifest in your career as you train several young employees, which leads to them having the skills and experience to launch their own businesses.

Does everyone fulfill their soul purpose?

The soul, while in Spirit, often overestimates the human potential.

There are instances where a soul is so eager to return to Earth from the Spirit realm that they leap into a childhood scenario before they see if the chosen environment will suit their needs. They may attempt their soul purpose, but without the skills and qualities, opportunities, and pivotal relationships they should have planned for.

While setting the goals for the next life, the soul is in an unlimited state, perhaps forgetting how difficult the challenges of living can be. Even though your soul has agreements with a powerful Spirit Team, you forget about them and rely only on yourself or other people. You insist on doing things the hard way, struggling alone, instead of letting your guides make things easier.

"Spirit will only give you what you can handle." A nice thought, but not always true. Instead, with your Spirit Team, "you can handle just about anything."

What keeps a person from their soul path?

You will be afraid to embrace your soul path if other attempts at being your full self have resulted in loss of love, mistreatment, making mistakes, or other failures. Following are some common false beliefs, examples of holding on to the wrong message after an experience:

"It's not fair for me to thrive while others are suffering." You may be sailing along, with clear focus on your path and cooperation with the team. Each step of the way feels blessed as you meet exactly the right person to launch you more quickly in the right direction, your efforts are met with enthusiasm, and you are swirling in the abundance of reciprocal energy (money is coming to you for being what you have come here to be). Then you begin to feel the wind taken out of your sails.

The person you are close to is not experiencing the same. They may have more trouble holding the vision or being on their path, or their lack of effort in overcoming the earlier soul growth and balancing keeps them struggling with their own goals and dreams. Your expansion into a more evolved way of operating in life has created a separation. They are not able to communicate clearly about what they are feeling, "Hey! You left me behind!"

What do you do? Do you shift your focus to the other, to the human drama, so that they will not suffer alone? Or do you keep going, knowing that you are on the right track for yourself and hope that your advances light the way for the other?

It is not unfair or selfish for you to succeed while others are struggling. You are more able to assist them when you take care of yourself. Your failure will not help them.

"What if people hate me? What if something bad happens?" When you were a child, you were unafraid to express the fullness of your exalted soul, the joy of being. Then you learned that others were sometimes unhappy unless you reigned yourself in. You were told not to, or sent to your room. Others may have treated you badly when you excelled, being envious of your talents. Your childhood training was toughening you up, *not* telling you to stop using your gifts.

In past lives, as well, there are residual memories of times when you were treated badly as you followed your true path. Perhaps you were persecuted for expressing ideas that challenged the established powers, robbed and killed for being wealthy, or abandoned by your tribe for unorthodox behavior. Your soul memory now warns, "You'll get punished unless you hold yourself back!"

Your past was designed to teach you balance – power *with* compassion, personal success with service to others – not to be less than you can be.

"What if I can't be trusted with greatness?" There are other lives where you have abused your strengths, for ego or power, losing sight of the purpose behind financial success, high station in life, intelligence, etc. You continue to see examples of imbalanced power all around you. These are the experiences that we all go through as we learn to appreciate the right use of power. Ask yourself, "If I was given all of the money in the world, what would I do with it?" If you answer, "build a castle on top of a mountain, fill it with riches, and make my servants do everything for me," you may need to look at your motives and fears. If your answer includes a plan that would benefit others as well as yourself, and do no harm, then have confidence that you can be trusted with becoming great.

"I am here to do this great thing. What if I fail?" You may see what you are here to do, and know how important your influence could be, but feel overwhelmed by the burden of responsibility. Do I have what it takes to achieve my vision? What if I am not good enough?

In a past life, a man came to present new technologies

for easier living, but was met with superstition and cast out of his community. He persisted in his goal, only occasionally being listened to, but not ever seeing his ideas actualized. In the current life, he is resistant to sharing his inventions – once again his soul path – afraid that his efforts would be futile.

It is not the results, but the effort that determines the success of a soul path. Embracing the opportunity to be what you have come here to be, no matter what the consequences, makes your life and soul purpose meaningful.

What can we do to step into a new consciousness instead of resisting our soul purpose?

You run into problems when you return to your human fears instead of staying focused on the soul vision. If your perspective is limited, future scenarios are formed from what has come before, instead of what could be *this* time.

Turn to creating a new possibility, a new outcome. Imagine that instead of receiving negative repercussions as you achieve your full potential, people around you are capable of embracing your success with shared joy.

It is time to retrain your system. Acknowledge what the feelings are about – warning signals – and tell your system a new story. "I release my fear of the past being repeated. My life is different now. I am stronger and smarter than before. It is safe for me to be successful and happy."

Imagine the people close to you – the loved one who pulls you back, the struggling child, the ailing parent, the coworker who undermines your work, the jealous friend. Recognize their insecurities, and see their need. Hold the vision that they are being supported by their own Spirit Team and shifting out of pain. See how they become self-confident and enthusiastic as they receive everything they need – acceptance, wisdom, strength and health.

See them being successful and happy. Imagine them as they could be, fulfilling their potential. Allow a new sensation to fill your being. See them overjoyed at good things happening to you. Embrace this feeling as your new soul memory, and the one you had since childhood can go away.

What's really wild is … You are such a magical being, and the vision can be so strong, that this new feeling gets sent out like radio waves and effects the other person as well.

Anyone would much rather feel the vibration of powerful harmony than the vibration of what was previously coming to them from you – repulsion – "I wish they'd leave me alone." (If you have the agenda that *they* have to change in order for you to feel good, then what they receive is your uncomfortable dislike.)

Hold this new vision for them, without attachment to what happens. It's an extremely powerful thing.

How does my Spirit Team help me with my specific soul purpose?

In general, they help you through your life, showing up as you go through challenges, leading you to opportunities, making sure you do not get too far away from addressing your goals. With their supportive energy, they give you courage to embrace your path, and with their otherworldly wisdom and magic, they add potency to your special gifts and talents.

If your soul purpose is to bring people together, your most potent Spirit Team helper may be your Networker, bringing you an extraordinary knack for knowing who needs to connect with whom, and why. But if you are focused on a healer path, perhaps as a nurse, your Body Healer will be the most instrumental in a practical way, as an avenue to access modern medical and alternative treatments as well as ancient knowledge.

There is also a potent shift, a change in the way you operate, through the connection, just by having their unlimited essence present in your life.

Your Spirit Team brings you the necessary qualities to achieve your goal. For instance, prior to becoming a Spirit guide, Constance (as a person) demonstrated stability, honesty and grounded wisdom in a past life with Beth. In this life, Beth needs those same qualities to pursue a path as a teacher. Even without conscious awareness, Beth naturally trusts the energy of Constance, as her Wise Protector in this life, especially during times when she could not trust herself. Through her "practice" with this guide, she eventually embodies those qualities for herself.

Coming across a soul from a past life, can cause you to re-experience the pain or fear generated by that traumatic memory, simply by association. Similarly, but with the opposite effect, being reconnected with a Spirit Team soul brings the feeling you had during a *harmonious* past life connection. Your Spirit Team members have been with you in a life, or two, where you were loved and honored as you achieved your full soul potential. To come into relationship with any of them again restores a sense of "rightness" in embracing your soul path and the memory of what is possible.

As you envision any of your Spirit Team, imagine your-self with them, as two people, in a past life. Imagine being back in time, in a place that seems unreal and magical, or vividly familiar. See it in detail, with whatever visuals come to mind as exactly perfect. See what the world is like, what role they play, and how you interact with them. Who are you and what are you supposed to be doing?

Understand that in this vision, this remembering, you have no fear, no experience with failure. Imagine yourself, performing your tasks in a smooth and easy manner. Imagine people around you being completely comfortable with whatever you are doing. In fact, they smile and appreciate you, sometimes observing, sometimes assisting. See yourself being supported by the one who is now on your Spirit Team, as well as by other people around you. See how your success spreads to others. Feel how it is to be loved and rewarded for being all that you have come here to be.

Remember, and hold this memory in your being.

This is the way of living that is open to you now. You are a soul, immense and potent, actualizing a journey in a physical form, supported by the unlimited power of your team.

Embrace the wildest of possibilities. What do you have to lose?

ACKNOWLEDGMENTS

Throughout my journey of discovering, exploring, doubting, fearing, practicing, testing and trusting, there have been many helpers. Without them, I would still be who I was before I started writing this book.

I give gratitude and thanks...

To Paula and Sandy, the wheels that rolled me out of my divorce crisis, for believing in the magic of Taliana's guidance before I did.

To Ema, whose desperation to change was the driving force behind hours of questions, and who used the information well, encouraging us both.

To Larry, who initiated the written compilation of a multitude of intelligent and universal questions.

To Ellen, who prodded me to publish by telling me that to keep this information to myself was criminal!

To Judy, who spread the word, connected me with ongoing clients, and eventually led me to my soulmate.

To Gillian, who has always been willing and able to blast me out of funks and delusions with hilarious in-my-face reality checks.

ABOUT THE AUTHOR

Daeryl Holzer is a clairvoyant and spiritual teacher who has been helping countless people to become more aware and empowered. With an uncommon compassion and insight, she shares techniques for discovering the underlying cause of challenges and for developing a deeper understanding of life from the soul perspective. Using visualizations and inspirational ways to "trick the brain," she has developed a unique and powerful system for transforming unhealthy feelings and actions into more harmonious and effective ones.

Since 1996, Daeryl has worked with individuals and small groups throughout the country, in person, by phone and email, as well as presenting lectures and workshops. Originally from the west coast states of California and Oregon, she now travels extensively from her desert home in far west Texas.

To inquire about personal sessions, book orders or upcoming events, please visit www.soulshift.com, or write to Daeryl Holzer, P.O. Box 1496, Marfa, TX 79843.